LENTEN
Adventure

David Rhodes is an Anglican priest attached to the city-centre team parish in Leeds and Chaplain Missioner of The Children's Society. For a number of years he worked for the ecumenical project 'Faith in Leeds', helping suburban churches to engage with social justice issues such as homelessness and poverty. A former national newspaper journalist, he has done extensive communications work for the Church Urban Fund, and is the author of *Faith in Dark Places* and the best-selling *Advent Adventure* (both Triangle).

*Dedicated to Mamphela Ramphele, formerly
Vice Chancellor of the University of Cape Town
and now Managing Director at the World Bank,
and to Steve Biko (1946–77) in thanksgiving
for their courage and inspiring commitment
to freedom, love and justice.*

LENTEN
Adventure

Daily Reflections from
Ash Wednesday to Easter Day

DAVID RHODES

Published in Great Britain in 2000 by
Society for Promoting Christian Knowledge
Holy Trinity Church
Marylebone Road
London NW1 4DU

Biblical extracts are from the Revised English Bible © Oxford
University Press and Cambridge University Press 1961, 1970;
and from the Revised Standard Version © 1946, 1952 and 1971 by the
Division of Christian Education of the National Council of the
Churches of Christ in the USA. Used by permission. All rights reserved.

British Library Cataloguing-in-Publication Data

A catalogue record for this book is available from the
British Library

ISBN 0-281-05319-7

Typeset by Pioneer Associates (Graphic) Ltd, Perthshire
Printed in Great Britain by
The Cromwell Press, Trowbridge, Wiltshire

Contents

CONTENTS

Foreword

It is customary during Lent to seek to immerse ourselves in the life story of Jesus. The 40-day period from Ash Wednesday to Holy Week echoes his time spent in the wilderness confronting the choices before him in his ministry. But other key moments are traced in the set Bible readings for this period. They culminate in the narrative leading up to his betrayal, death and resurrection. David Rhodes calls us into this deeply traditional activity – but in a startling, contemporary way – by setting the story of Jesus alongside his encounters with an unusual company of people from the underside of today's respectable society. People we would not normally expect to be the bearers of religious truth or insight.

The central pathway through the book is the Lord's Prayer. Each week *Lenten Adventure* takes one of the comfortable phrases of this much-loved prayer and renders it dangerous again. The result is some arresting juxtapositions which intrigue and surprise – and sometimes shock. But they are authentic to the Gospel in a way you can't miss. And, like the gospel narratives, they hang in the memory.

Lent books, and this is no exception, are typically divided into quite short sections to be read each day. You might suppose the point of this is to tempt the busy reader to tackle something that demands only a small space in their day. But actually the opposite is true. The format is specially designed to be read slowly – for only one chunk a day to be absorbed.

I don't know about you, but my days are clogged with printed text that I have to read and then discard fast. The newspaper is scanned today and binned tomorrow. Its messages, no matter how troubling, cannot be allowed to touch too deeply. My e-mails have to be dealt with and deleted quickly to clear my desk. And the world is everywhere inscribed with adverts that annoy or amuse and which I try not to believe.

But this book I need to take slowly. The reading process makes quite a different use of time, consciously re-ordering it and giving my soul the space to catch up with my brain and my eyes. *Lenten Adventure* asks not to be dealt with and deleted, it asks to be lingered over and remembered.

The problem is that David Rhodes is such a good story-teller that you want to read on. Every day the passage seems to stop too soon. The discipline is not to start reading but to agree to stop. You have to give the stories time to sink in: living with them through the activities of your day and sleeping with them at night. Only then can they enter your own story, and the adventure begin.

Janet Morley

Introduction

The simple things in life are often the most important. There is a delightfully simple story in the gospels about Jesus walking along the seashore. He sees some men in a fishing boat. It is a scene of peace and tranquillity. He calls out to them: Come with me and I will show you a different sort of fishing. A simple invitation: Follow me.

We do not know whether there was any discussion. All we know is that the two fishermen followed him. They left their boat on the shore and walked with him along the beach into the greatest adventure of their lives. In that moment of decision, with the sun glistening on the sea, they said yes. And nothing was ever the same again.

As fishermen, they had often cast off and sailed into the unknown, never knowing what the weather might do or whether they would catch anything. Now they were casting off and walking into the unknown. They did not know it, but the future would bring them laughter and pain – and it would bring death. All they knew at that moment was they were embarking on an adventure.

Like those fishermen, and the other disciples who were to walk with them, we too are being invited to set out on an adventure. We are being called by the same person who stood on the seashore and called them. We are being gently challenged to make that same simple decision. We are being invited to take part in a great adventure. It will bring us laughter and pain – and it will bring us life.

Day by day on this pilgrimage through Lent we will listen, explore and reflect on what God is saying to us. During our journey we will be guided by the Lord's Prayer. Each week a single phrase from that deep and dangerous prayer will be our guide until we arrive at last in the pain and turmoil of Holy Week and the cross. And, perhaps, glimpse something more.

Our companions in this adventure will be the gospel writers.

We will listen to their words as truthfully as we can but, to uncover the implications of that truth, we will also try to picture and understand the situations in which the gospel events took place. We will not just think about what people did, but why they may have acted in that way – and try to uncover some of the fears and passions which drove them.

This is not a book of scientific analysis, although we have a deep respect for biblical research. Instead, it is like sitting before a great painting in whose brushstrokes we begin to discern a powerful, emerging truth.

We will also walk with companions from our own time and our own neighbourhoods. We will hear the stories of people of courage and wisdom. Some of them are unlikely companions: people who have been damaged and abused; people who are homeless and unemployed. People whose lives hang by a thread. Little people in the world's reckoning, but people of the Kingdom. The sort of people Jesus knew and loved. There is heart-breaking pain and deep laughter in these stories, but that does not matter. What matters is that there is life.

Day 1   Week 1
ASH WEDNESDAY
The Clergy Sponsored Swim

Water is a great leveller. Especially swimming pool water. That was the real attraction of the clergy sponsored swim. After years of raising money for Christian Aid, our clergy group were running out of new ideas. The house-to-house collections were the bedrock of our support, but for years we had organized all manner of other events – sponsored walks, pancake bakes, sponsored car washing. But that was all in the past. What we needed now was something different, and the clergy must give the lead.

Who among our congregations would not pay good money to see the vicar in his swimming trunks? And so they did. Hundreds of them. The swimming baths felt chill that evening as the vicar and Harry, the Methodist minister, and other reluctant participants got changed. Never had Anglican–Methodist unity been stronger as the two ministers led the clergy out for their moment of truth. Never had a crowd cheered gladiators with more glee than on that cold evening. Those about to die of misery, salute you.

For once, questions of doctrine and theology were forgotten. Each length would bring more help to Christian Aid. And, for the vicar, unexpected embarrassment.

In a welcome show of solidarity with their clergy, people from the different congregations had also volunteered to swim. Among them was Corinne, a young woman with Down's Syndrome. She was often at the pool and would take great delight in going down the water slide. She occasionally swam across the pool, but little more. Taking part in the sponsored swim, she was not a serious participant but she had been welcomed as a much-loved member of her church. 'Two pounds a length,' the vicar said. 'Well done!'

And so it was. She swam a length. And then another. Then a third. At 14 lengths the vicar realized she was easily keeping pace with him in the pool. He tried to call out encouragingly but choked on a mouthful of water. She laughed and waved. At 16 lengths she knew all was not well with him. He was slowing perceptibly: 'Pull,

1

pull,' she called encouragingly across the pool as though he were an oarsman. But it was too late. He was dragged ashore and retired to change.

Some time later he reappeared on the pool-side seats to a ripple of applause from the spectators. Meanwhile, in the water, the swimming continued and, as it did, an uncomfortable realization began to dawn on the vicar. 'How many lengths has Corinne swum now?' he asked uneasily. 'Forty-two, so far,' came the reply. Forty-two lengths. Eighty-four pounds. And still she swam. 'Come on,' they cried. 'Come out,' he bawled. At last she did, but only because it was time to close the pool.

They met outside on the pavement in a crowd of swimmers and spectators. Throwing her arms round him she said, 'You were terrible!' Yes, he thought, but I've learnt a lot tonight. It was not the first time that God had used her to teach him a gentle lesson.

—•—

Water seems to be a favourite teaching medium for God. The story of Lent begins with it – in fact it begins in it. And, like the vicar, we too may learn a profound lesson.

After centuries of seeming silence, the voice of God was heard again. But it was not a gentle voice. According to St Matthew, the man we know as John the Baptist was rough in appearance and rough in manner. Dressed in a primitive coat of camel skin tied with a leather belt, he lived outside the towns and villages in the wilderness on a diet of locusts and wild honey. At last the voice of the prophet was heard in the land – a challenging, uncomfortable, uncompromising voice which spoke the word of God.

And the word was not one of praise and congratulation. It was a word of anger and warning. Repent, for the Kingdom of God is upon you – the powerful presence of God's rule is close to you. But, despite his rough tongue, the people came to him. In their hundreds they came, from town and city. But when some of the clergy appeared, John became incandescent with rage. 'You vipers' brood! Who warned you to escape from the coming retribution?' he roared. But still they came.

What were all those people doing there? They were coming to this wild and turbulent man called John because they knew there was a problem. And their problem was with God. Despite being the 'children' of God, as they described themselves, they knew their relationship with God was in serious trouble. John also knew they were in trouble and, despite his anger, he was offering them a way forward. It began with the acknowledgement that there was a problem. Come and be truthful, said John. Come and recognize you have damaged your relationship with God. Ask God to wash away that failure now.

And so it was they came to John to be baptized in the River Jordan. No matter how intelligent or wealthy or important – all went down into the levelling water to ask God to wash their failure and sinfulness away. They asked God; they did not ask John. John may have been standing alongside them in the water, but he was not standing in judgement on them.

It is to the eternal credit of John that he resisted the temptation to claim that power for himself. Instead of saying that he was the one who would bring in a new relationship of life and hope, a new understanding of God, he had the honest humility to point to someone else. 'There is one who comes after me who is mightier than I am,' said John. 'And I am not fit to take off his shoes. I baptize you with water but he will baptize you with the Holy Spirit . . .'

Then comes a moment in which we almost hear the laughter of God. For among the crowd John suddenly sees the very person about whom he is speaking. The question is: Will Jesus now baptize John in the Jordan?

He does not. Instead Jesus asks John to baptize him. In that moment of wonderful confusion John, for once, does not know what to do. 'I cannot baptize you,' he tells Jesus in alarm, 'It is you who should be baptizing me.'

But Jesus gently insists. 'Let it be so for the present,' he tells John. 'We do well to conform in this way to what God requires.'

Struggling to comprehend what is happening, John agrees and Jesus goes down into the water to be baptized. Picture that moment, frozen in time. John gently lowers Jesus under the surface of the river in baptism and the water closes over his head. John, in that moment, looks across the river at the faces of the astonished crowds and, in that eternity of stillness, can say nothing.

What was there to say? How could this person, who we believe to be the human expression of God's nature and will, be baptized? Baptism means a turning away from sin and failure – failure of relationship with God. Failure to allow ourselves to accept God's love and to love God in return. John knows this cannot be true for the person who he is at that very moment raising up out of the water, back into the world.

Did Jesus feel in need of the washing of baptism? What was going on? Did this change the nature of baptism? Was baptism no longer about the recognition of past mistakes and failure? Or was something else being learnt – that baptism is a sign of our relationship with God; and that relationship involves trust. Not just the trust that God is with us like the reassuring presence of an insurance policy in case of trouble, but a trust that surrenders control to God. In baptism we are not only washed as a sign of God's loving forgiveness, we are also submerged in his life-giving love. And that is a frightening risk.

Perhaps Jesus knew how important it was to stand alongside the people in their sinful human condition and to share with them in their response to God's love. First, by physically lowering himself into the water of the Jordan, but also by showing them the need to surrender to God. Perhaps that incidental moment in which the baptized person goes under the water and disappears for a few seconds from the face of the earth is crucially important. Are we willing to disappear? To not be? Are we willing to submerge our own agenda and desires, even for a moment, for God?

That baptism was one which John did not expect but perhaps he discovered in that dramatic event something new about God's involvement in the world. That to find God we sometimes need not look up. Instead we need to look around – or sometimes down to people we may think are below us.

John probably found that extremely hard to comprehend. Even people who have great book learning and who have been trained in theology still cannot explain what was really happening. But I suspect Corinne would understand.

Day 2   Week 1
THURSDAY
Money Makes Us Hungry

It was raining and we were lost. Somewhere on a long-distance walk called the Dales Way we had taken a wrong turn. The path running from the Yorkshire Dales to the Lake District is well marked – unless it is foggy and pouring down with that relentless rain that only falls in England in August.

Our clothes and rucksacks were soaked; our boots heavy with mud. Across the field, so the guide book said, was a stile. There was no stile. In the mist we could not see the other side of the field. The rain was so heavy it was hard to see anything except the cows that loomed out of the mist, large and uncomfortably close.

We had walked for hours. Lunch time had passed and we had forgotten to bring any Mars bars. Alan, my walking companion, went ahead as always. He is an inch taller than I am. Never, ever go walking with someone taller than you are. They walk faster. I was hungry and no food was in sight. No café was in sight – no village was in sight. Nothing was in sight except a lot of wet grass. We walked for hours. Days. It felt like 40 days. And still there was no shop. No food.

Eventually we came to a road. Alan consulted the map. 'There's a village,' he said.

'Where?'

'Just down the road.'

'How far down the road?'

'About a mile.'

The hunger increased with every step. I thought about stories of people sucking a pebble to ease the anguish of hunger or thirst. But the only pebbles I could see were coated in wet mud.

At last we came to the tiny village. It was almost four in the afternoon, but the single street was deserted. Rainwater sluiced down the gutters. No matter. There ahead of us was the village shop. I could taste the food – the tuna sandwiches, donuts, chocolate bars, ice cream. Alan stopped. At first I did not catch what he said. He said it again. 'Half-day closing.' And still it rained.

—◦—

In the desert it was not raining. But the man was hungry. He had walked alone for days. It seemed like 40 days. Or 40 years. He could hardly remember a time when he had not been alone in the dry waste. He did not know whether he was lost. It hardly mattered. He was so hungry he felt like lying down in the dust and dying. Why was he there? What was he looking for? An answer? A meaning? Wanting to be close to God, open to God, exposed to God, he had left the town and walked. And walked.

In the silence of the desert, there had been nothing between him and God. He could listen to the sound of God, feel the closeness of God. Sense the awesome moving of God. But that had been days ago. Since then he had felt only hunger. At first it was only the hint of desire for food but now, a knotting hunger which stopped him sleeping at night and once awake, stopped him thinking. Almost stopped him praying.

In the half-light of the morning, crouching below an overhang of rock, the stones around him caught the first hint of sunrise and must have seemed for all the world like light brown loaves of new-baked bread. And in his ear he heard a voice which whispered soft and comforting words: Why not?

Why not, if you are so hungry? You have the power. Could you not say the word, and these stones would indeed become bread? If you are who you sense and feel you are. If you are the one in whom God dwells. If you are the one to whom is given power. Why not? What is power if not to be used? Have you come here to die? Why not, my friend? Why not? The shop door was open. He had only to take that one small step inside.

Why not? Why did he say no to such a tempting offer? It sounds so brave and noble to resist temptation; to set aside power, even for a moment. But perhaps he sensed another voice which said: Will you not trust me one more day?

—◦—

Will you not trust me? We too are faced with that question as we begin our own journey through Lent, and in each day of our lives. We too are given power. Whether it is cash, the plastic credit card, intelligence or influence – we have power in the world. Power to buy. Power to feed our hunger for security and status.

How hard it is to set aside our power, even for a moment. To let go of that commodity which gives us so much comfort – money. How easy it is to spend that money on ourselves and, with each purchase, build up a wall of secure protection from the world. Or buy ourselves the recognition of our neighbours who read the signals of our wealth and power and welcome us as members of the club. How hard it is to give a few small coins to charity. The questions that small gesture triggers: Will this money be wasted? How much will go in overheads? Are these people really needy or am I being conned? What have they to do with me? I do not know you.

We seldom realize how the money magic works. It is a conjuror's trick of great simplicity, but so convincing. The trick of money is that it appears to place us at the centre. It says, Buy this – why not? Possess this – why not? Be this – why not? Money works by persuading us we are the controller, the master, the centre. As though our money worships us.

But the reality is the opposite. Money is the measure of our lives. The numbers on it tell us so. Few other commodities come with numbers on. But money does. And numbers make us hungry. Numbers make us compete. If others have more, then we have less and money tells us we are less. And we want more. And so we work and fight and cheat and steal for more. Our meaning is measured by the index of success and money. It seems that money is the god who feeds our hunger. But it is a false god because the hunger never lessens.

Read the papers – people with more millions than they can count or comprehend are driven by a hunger for more and yet more money. The addiction is total. The servitude is complete. The god of money is worshipped.

But did the Christ person not say: 'Render unto Caesar what rightfully belongs to Caesar and unto God what rightfully belongs to God?' For centuries that quotation has been used to justify power and greed. An excuse for separating what belongs to God and what belongs to the world. To Mammon. Did no one hear the dark humour in his voice when he spoke those words? Did no one ever ask the simple question: What rightfully belongs to God?

Had no one read the Psalms and heard the words: 'How fearful is the Lord Most High; great sovereign over all the earth' and 'Thou has fixed the earth immovable; from all eternity thou art God.'

Render unto God that which is God's. But what is there in all creation that does not belong to the Creator? What do we have which is not held in trust from God? Whether or not Jesus was telling his listeners to pay their taxes is open to debate. What is not in dispute is that all we have and all we are is a gift from God and rightfully belongs to God. Our worship and our lives are nothing more than the living out of the statement: All things come from you, Lord, and of your own do we give you. God is at the centre and God holds everything in being in a great, ongoing act of creation.

Out there in the desert the issue was not one of bread. No matter how hungry the man felt, he was not being tempted to eat. The bread was only the bait. He was being tempted to place self at the centre and to turn away from God. The deception was that by doing so, he would live. It was a powerful argument. But the man knew it was untrue. We are alive in God; in the trust that says, no matter how desperately hungry I am for food or for security or for significance, I will be true to you – for one more day. For one more baptism moment. Even if I die, I will be true to you.

He did not die that day, but he knew the day when death would come was not far off. In the meantime the soft voice of the tempter would return many times. And the next time would be tomorrow.

———◆———

FRIDAY

All that Glitters

Have you ever thought how odd it is that the best-known book in the world does not have a title? The words 'the Bible' simply mean 'books' which is a bit unimaginative. No doubt it is too late in the day to start thinking of a better name for this large collection of documents which make up the bedrock of the Christian faith. *Tales of the Unexpected* might have been a possible contender.

The Bible is the story of God's dealings with men and women and, from beginning to end, it is the story of the unexpected. Our traditional images of the Church and of the Bible suggest everything is rather predictable and boring, but the reality is that the Bible is full of surprises. It is just that we do not always hear what it is saying to us.

Not only is the Bible full of surprises, the story of the Church is also the story of the unexpected. None more unexpected than the story of how the Church became accepted as the religion of the Roman empire.

For centuries the fledgling Church had suffered persecution from successive Roman emperors. This became even more violent after the secular emperors began to style themselves as gods. Roman subjects were then required to 'worship' the emperor god. Many probably crossed their fingers and did as they were told. For Christians, however, this was a crucial matter of principle. There was one God and they would worship no one else. But, in addition to being an act of spiritual rebellion, this was also politically subversive. If a small group of Christians were going to disobey the Roman emperor and get away with it, then others might be tempted to do the same. Ferocious persecution followed.

The strange thing was that the persecution did not kill off the Church, or its spirit of loving obedience to God. The prisons were bursting at the seams with Christians and still the emperor did not get his way. How those Christians must have prayed for an end to their suffering, and perhaps prayed the emperor might himself

9

become a Christian. How wonderful if the whole empire could be united under the loving rule of Jesus Christ.

Then, rather like the Berlin Wall coming down, it happened. The emperor became a Christian. This true 'tale of the unexpected' happened in the year 311 when Constantine the Great was about to fight a major battle. Outnumbered by the enemy, the story goes, he saw in the sky the sign of the cross and the words 'In this sign, conquer.' And conquer he did. In the following year he defeated his rival Maxentius after marching on Rome and, ten years later, came his victory over his one remaining rival, Licinius, at the Battle of the Bosphorus. Constantine was sole ruler of the empire – and he was a Christian.

The conversion of Constantine was one of the greatest and most unexpected events in the history of the Church. But, looking back, many people believe its effect on the worshipping community was disastrous. The moment the emperor became a Christian, huge numbers of the rich and powerful, politicians and diplomats – anyone interested in furthering their own interests – followed suit. Often, regardless of what they believed.

The Church ceased to be a persecuted minority and, instead, became the official religion of the most powerful political system on earth. People signed up in their thousands to receive their religious passport to success. As a result of all this, huge sums of money were poured into building churches and shrines. The bishops, once called the overseers of the poor, became princes of the state entitled to wear the royal purple and to live in luxury in palaces. A large slab of tax revenue was channelled into the Church's coffers; an amount so vast that, years later when it was cut to a third of its original size, it was still extremely generous. It was a church treasurer's dream come true.

But all was not well. What at first seemed a wonderful change for the better became, for many people, an unexpected change for the worse. The Church had come close to ruling the world, but in doing so had lost its soul. Power replaced prayerfulness; worldly success became its inner failure.

◄●►

In this story we hear an echo of another tale of the unexpected. A story where once more there had been the promise of power and authority – the opportunity to rule the world. The old enemy took Jesus to a high place, a mountain top. Spread out below them were all the nations of the world.

Altitude does strange things to the human mind. It helps greatly when people are asked to drop bombs on other people – houses become little more than tiny dots on a patchwork landscape below. Unable to recognize the people below them or to look into their faces, it is relatively easy to press the button.

People sitting begging in the streets of Britain are looked down upon by people passing by in more ways than one. We look down on them physically because they are below us on the pavement. We look down on them socially because they are not always as well dressed as we are; we look down on them in their humanity by using degrading terms such as 'the poor' or 'the underclass' or 'the drop-out'.

—◦—

One day a church worker involved with homeless people was sitting in the congregation at a service in a city-centre church. As he sat listening to the reading, a homeless man came and sat beside him. He knew what would happen next – the homeless man, finding a captive audience, would beg some money. He waited in anticipation for the question of money to be raised.

Sure enough, after a few minutes, the homeless man leaned across. 'Here,' he said, 'I can't stay. Will you put this in the collection for me? They often give me sandwiches at this church and I just want to say thank you.' He pressed two pound coins into the church worker's hand and slipped away. Looking down on other people, it is so easy to think we know best.

—◦—

Standing on that mountain top looking down on the world, there must have been a huge temptation for Jesus to think he knew best. How alluring it must have been to think how the power he had been given could be used to rule the world. And who better to do it?

I can give you all this, says the old enemy. Together we can control all of creation. You and me, together. You worship me and I reward you with all this. Just say the word. If Jesus did share our humanity and if he was tempted on the mountain top and on the cross to save himself, then here is someone we can relate to at the deepest level of our own needs.

No matter how small and insignificant other people seem when we look down on them from the mountain top of power and social superiority, when we stand alongside them – or sit alongside them in a city-centre church – we see our neighbour. A person deeply loved by God.

But is God there? And how can we be sure? That was the third and most awesome question that Jesus had to face in his loneliness. Am I dreaming all this? Is God really with me? How could he be sure? The third temptation came up with the answer.

———◆———

Day 4 Week 1
SATURDAY
THE SMALL MIRACLE

Today, though most people are unaware of it, a small miracle is happening. In one of the back streets of what is called the inner city, a removal van has pulled up. Neighbours peer silently from behind their curtains and, down in the street, a small group of children and a dog gather to watch. Eve is moving house. And, though few people watching are aware of it, what is happening is nothing short of a miracle.

The story began many years ago. Eve's parents separated when she was a child. Eventually her mother remarried. At first things seemed normal, but then the nightmare began. One day when Eve came home from school, her stepfather took her upstairs in their comfortable middle-class house. He took her clothes off. Then he took photographs of her, then he raped her. She was ten years old. Over the next few years Eve was sexually abused many times by the man she had been told she must trust – and by several of his friends.

Traumatized by her ordeal, Eve was then prostituted by her stepfather. For the next 15 years she continued to live a life of prostitution. Then, a few years ago, the miracle began to happen. An unusual event called a poverty hearing was being held in the city. This was a chance for people living in situations of poverty and insecurity to speak about their life experiences to an audience of the great and the good – civic leaders, company directors and others in positions of power and influence. Eve, who had been helped by a church project set up to help prostituted women, was asked to speak.

What she had to say was so powerful that she was invited to go to London to speak at the National Poverty Hearing. In the audience was the Archbishop of Canterbury, George Carey, and the Catholic Archbishop of Westminster, Cardinal Basil Hume. Again, Eve's story and her powerful picture of life on the streets of Britain stunned her listeners.

'Two thirds of prostitutes have been abused as children,' she told them. 'Prostitution is not about fulfilling sexual fantasies – it is about abuse. It is about poverty. Take a good look at me. Next time you see a prostitute, you do not see a whore – you see a survivor. You do not see child prostitutes – you see prostituted children.'

When she had finished, Cardinal Hume stood up: 'That courageous woman is my sister,' he said.

After the hearing, the Archbishop of Canterbury had a long conversation with Eve – a conversation which was to have a remarkable outcome. Going home, Eve thought about what had happened. She had been listened to with respect by an archbishop and by a cardinal. She was invited by a woman priest to start going to her local church. She asked another priest she trusted to be her spiritual director. She started working for a church project among vulnerable young children in her own neighbourhood.

As her faith grew deeper, an amazing idea began to develop. No one can remember who first had the courage to put it into words, but it was something we all felt. Eve went to see her vicar: 'I think I am being called to the priesthood,' she said. She waited for the laughter but there was none.

'Yes, I've had the same thought,' said the vicar.

We sat down and thought about the impossible idea which was staring us all in the face. It was simply crazy. It might be true to the Gospel with its stories of Christ's love for the poor, the outcast and the prostituted – but you do not expect the Gospel to happen in real life. Perhaps that is the trouble with the Church today.

Some months later, Eve went to see the bishop. He was a tall and patrician figure, academic and dignified. It is unlikely he had ever met a prostitute in his life. Coming from a different world, it seemed he would have nothing in common with Eve. But we were wrong. They did have something in common – a deep trust in God. Confronted by this courageous and articulate woman whose childhood had been a living nightmare and whose adult life was as far from that of the average churchgoer as it was possible to imagine, the bishop had a very difficult choice to make. Should he allow her to go to college to train for ordination as a priest in the Church of Christ? He said yes.

That is why the removal van came today. This is the day Eve left the terraced back street where she has lived for the past five years and set off to study at a theological college. But it was not easy. The courageous young woman, who stood up in front of an audience of 500 people – including two archbishops – and spoke with a powerful integrity about life on the streets, this woman was now suddenly feeling afraid and unsure.

Was this for real? Was she dreaming? Was God really calling her to be a priest? Or was this simply madness? Was she being tempted to make the most public and humiliating mistake of her life? How much easier to tell the removal men to put the furniture back in the house – to close the door, and to forget about God. How much she needed at that moment to know beyond all doubt that God was with her. How comforting it would have been to be able to prove that God was with her – to put God to the test.

—◆—

Out in the desert, Eve's friend was feeling much the same way. He was a carpenter from a small northern town. What was he doing out there in the desert wandering around trying to listen to God's voice? Was this for real – or was he, too, dreaming? How much easier to walk back the way he had come and go home. Back to the workbench, to the plane and the chisel, the sawdust and safety. How much he needed to know that God was with him. How comforting it would be to have an absolute guarantee that God was there; to put God to the test.

And in his ear he heard the voice again. This time it said: 'If you are the Son of God, throw yourself down from this topmost pinnacle of the Temple. See how God will instantly send his angels to save you.' What could be easier? All you have to do is jump. Why not? If God loves you and wants you to do this work for him? Why not? Prove it.

But the man could see the trap that was being set. To test God is to try to control God and to do violence to the trust which is at the heart of love. To seek proof would be to degrade and abuse that relationship, just as surely as prostitution is an abuse of a child or adult.

—◆—

Relationships of trust and love are what make us human. But such things are never easy. Trust and love make us vulnerable. We are no longer in control; and sometimes we get hurt. Perhaps that is one reason why men abuse and prostitute women and young children – sexual and physical violence is easier than love. And the abuser seldom gets hurt.

In her childhood, Eve was often hurt. Looking back, it seems a miracle she ever survived her ordeal at the hands of her stepfather and the other men. But, instead of being destroyed by her experience, she grew up to be a woman of courage and integrity – and a wisdom beyond her years.

How tempting it must have been to seek a quiet life in her local community. To work for her church and enjoy security and modest comfort. But setting out in that removal van, she is well aware that ahead lies the way of danger and still more pain. She knows what will happen when the newspapers get the story of the 'holy hooker' and when people in the Church look down on her disdainfully, as they surely will, and there are the whispers of condemnation. For we always blame the abused and not the abuser.

But she is away on her journey and in the desert her friend is also moving on. Not back to the safety and comfortable predictability of his home town and his family, but out into the unknown where there is doubt and uncertainty. Where the holy people will look down on him disdainfully; where there will be first the whispers and then the shouts of condemnation. And one day they will have their way and it will end on a hillside with a death. And I fear for Eve, that they will crucify her, too. But she has made her choice and she walks the way of the cross. And on that journey she will spark in people the deep realization of the love of God. Although she cannot prove it, that is her calling. Scared and uncertain, she has set out on another stage in her journey of faith.

And that is what we are trying to do this Lent. God called Eve from the streets of the city and, just as surely, he is calling you and me today. But do we have the courage and the integrity to make that journey? Given the temptation to close our hearts to that invitation it will be a miracle if we do – but miracles still happen. And we have good people going on ahead of us.

FIRST SUNDAY OF LENT
The High-Wire Act

If you are one of those people who enjoy being scared by horror films or the thrill of the big wheel at the leisure park, you should try visiting the Italian city of Turin. There you will find a strange building which looks rather like a Victorian red-brick skyscraper. No one is quite sure why it was built. It has no obvious purpose other than being a tourist attraction. There is an observation platform at the top with spectacular views over the city hundreds of feet below. There is, of course, a lift from ground level. And that is when things get frightening. There may be a warning printed in very small type in Italian on your ticket to the top, but there are no large signs saying you are about to have the shock of your life.

What happens to the unsuspecting tourist is simply this: You walk off the street into the entrance lobby and buy a ticket to the observation platform. You walk into the lift and press the button. The door closes and you start going up. As you leave the ground floor level, however, you suddenly realize this enormous tower has no floors in it. It is completely empty, a shell of a building. Not only that, the lift walls and ceiling are made of clear glass.

You find yourself suspended by a very thin wire, in mid-air, in a huge empty space. The other people in the lift look as though they do this every day – or they have read the small print on the ticket – or they are just cool Italians. Meanwhile, your heart has stopped beating and you know beyond all doubt you are going to die. You look up and there, far above you, is a pin-point of bright light from which the lift cable hangs. That is where you are going.

If you can get your eyes to focus, you look out across empty space to the walls of the square tower in which you are having this nightmare. All round you, there is nothing except the glass walls of the lift. It is quite hard to imagine how there can be such a thing as eternity – or how time can cease to matter. The journey in that lift is a good example of how time can stand still – or last forever.

Finally, after about a hundred years, the lift reaches the top. You stagger out on to the observation platform and stare dully down at the city you wish you had never visited. The air is fresh; the tourists chatter. But there is only one thing you can think of – sometime you are going to have to go back down in that glass lift.

What a good thing it is that most lifts are not designed that way. You cannot see out or down. Even so, it is a sobering thought just to imagine what is six inches beneath your feet when you take a lift to the tenth floor of a hospital or office block. But for most of us, snug in that little metal box, those troubling thoughts are far away; nothing disturbs our comfort as we are whisked to the top floor.

—•—

It may sound bizarre, but exactly the same process takes place when we pray. Whether by accident or design, we have somehow been taught that prayer is a comfortable and relaxing activity. As children, years ago, many of us were told to say our prayers before we got into bed. Or, in very cold weather before the invention of central heating, perhaps we could say them in bed. Wherever we said them, they were thought of as a gentle sedative to help us to sleep – God tucking us up for the night, a religious cup of cocoa.

For many of us, this continues into adult life and there is no better example of this spiritual sedative than the Lord's Prayer. It is so well known that we say the first two words and the rest of the prayer says itself. Like driving a car on a well-known route, we can be thinking of any number of other things while we are doing it. The Lord's Prayer has become a comfortable old settee to slump into at the end of the day; a soothing warm drink to be taken last thing at night. God's in his heaven and all is right with the world. God bless Mummy and Daddy and Florence the cat and help me to be a better boy. Hands together, eyes closed. We press the prayer button in the religious lift; there is the gentle hum of words and we are transported effortlessly to the end of our conversation with God. Conveniently, there is always the gentle bump of the Amen to let us know we have arrived at our floor. Then it is time to turn out the light and go to sleep.

What sacrilege! What blasphemy! What an abuse of God's love for us. What a complete and total deceit. Is it by chance that we close our eyes when we say our prayers? Is that to shut out the world? Or to shut out the reality of God? Perhaps we should examine just what is happening when we say the comfortable and familiar words of the Lord's Prayer.

First, we are acknowledging the existence and presence in our lives of the Creator of the whole universe. The awesome and overwhelming force that brought the speck of dust called the Earth into existence about 4,000 million years ago. We are reaching out and touching a high-voltage cable capable of turning the whole of creation to ash. We are speaking in the presence of the source of all meaning and purpose. We are not standing or kneeling in the cosy carpeted cabin of a luxury elevator in a high-rise office block. We are suspended in space a thousand million miles above anything that we can know or control. Hanging by a single word – grace.

Every second of our lives, we are held in existence by the gift of God's love. At any moment, we can cease to be. Life is God's gift to us at each moment of our existence. We look up and there, a million light years above us, is a pin-point of light, and that is where we are headed. There is no real prayer without fear – not at the anger of God but at the awesomeness of God and the amazing fact of God's love for us. Far from putting us gently to sleep at the end of the day, it is enough to keep us awake for every second of the night.

―●―

There is a story of an elderly woman who was having great trouble saying her prayers. She eventually spoke to her priest about it.

'What's the trouble?' he asked.

'Well,' said the woman, 'I start saying the Lord's Prayer and when I've said "Our Father" I can't get any further. I just can't stop thinking about how amazing those words are. I just keep turning them over in my mind.'

The priest smiled. 'I wish more people had your problem,' he said.

―●―

The problem for the rest of us is that we do not start thinking about how amazing those words are – or how dangerous they are. Did Jesus really know what he was doing when he taught his disciples to say those opening words? Of course he did, and he was not giving them a cup of religious cocoa. The first words of the Lord's Prayer are rather like a depth charge. For a moment nothing seems to happen. Then, if you are really praying, there comes the explosion. It comes, first, from the meaning of the words themselves – and, second, from the consequences of praying those words.

First, the word we translate as 'Our Father' is in fact the word 'Abba' in Aramaic, the language which Jesus spoke. 'Abba' does not quite mean 'father' if we take that to mean a dignified and distant patriarchal figure. The sense of the word is much more the intimate and familiar word 'daddy' which may be spoken in love and trust by a child. This does not mean it is a childish word, but it is a child-like word. It could be spoken by a very small child or by a teenager. The sense is not one of disrespect but of love, trust and intimacy.

The first shock wave from the explosion has just hit us. We are in the presence of the most awesome and powerful force in the universe. We are suspended on a thread of life and daring to address the God of all creation. And what do we say? 'Say Daddy,' Jesus tells his disciples. No wonder the elderly woman never got past the first word – she was struck dumb by the awesomeness of what she was being invited to say in the first words of the Lord's Prayer. How dare we say it? How can we even think it?

But if the first word raises huge questions about our relationship with God, it causes us just as many problems in our relationship with our neighbour. Why? Because the Lord's Prayer is one of the most revolutionary statements ever made. The political, social and economic implications are astounding. No wonder we hide ourselves away and shut our eyes tight when we say it. If we have the courage to speak the first word of the prayer, and believe what we are saying, then we are being challenged to change the world – as we will discover tomorrow.

Day 6   Week 2
MONENDAY
INTO THE UNKNOWN

As we turned off the motorway which led east out of Cape Town, we saw ahead of us down the dusty side road the corrugated iron shacks and temporary dwellings of a South African township. Old polythene bags caught in the barbed wire fence at the side of the road flapped furiously in the strong wind which blew across the sandy coastal plain. Ahead lay a squatter camp in which thousands of black South Africans clung on to life. Many had been evicted from the city years before by the white government and left here to live or die. Others had migrated here because of the even more extreme poverty in other areas.

Stories of township violence and killings came to mind. But it was too late to turn back. At that moment I wanted God to tell me I did not have to go to this strange and dangerous location called Guguletu. The beautiful city of Cape Town was only a few miles away along the motorway, but it seemed a different world. Foolishly, I had asked if I could stay for a few days with a family in a township to learn at first-hand something of the life of the black population of South Africa. It sounded an interesting idea. Now, confronted with the reality, it felt like madness. As we drove down the dusty streets, people turned to watch the conspicuously new car in which I was travelling. The place seemed to be electric with danger.

At last we reached the place where I was to stay. Not a squatter shack made of old packing cases and plastic sheeting, but a simple house. I was welcomed by an elderly and dignified man called Mr Soyekwa. I was to be his guest. Together with the people who had brought me from Cape Town, we sat at table and shared a good meal. The priest from the church, Mxolisi, had come with his wife. He sat at one end of the table and Mr Soyekwa sat at the other like two Old Testament prophets. As we ate, I could hear the noises of the township outside. The door was open but the wrought-iron security gate was closed. Some months before, Mr Soyekwa had been attacked by two armed youths who broke into his home and robbed him.

Finally it was time to go – for them but not for me. As my escorts drove away into the warm night, I felt a sudden panic and isolation. I felt like shouting for them to stop and take me with them, but it was too late. I was alone in a South African township staying with an elderly black person I had never met before.

Lying in bed that night, I could not sleep for the noise. Not the noise of passing cars or gunfire – the sound of the occasional car being driven at high speed was not much different from the inner-city area where I lived in England. And there did not seem to be any gunfire. What was keeping me awake was the wind which whipped across the coastal flatlands on which the township was built. We were in a house made of brick and with a substantial roof, but I could still feel the tremors as the wind buffeted the building. I thought about the people outside in the township. Many lived in secure brick or concrete houses, but thousands of others were living in makeshift shelters with no windows and no doors. How did they keep the sandy soil from blowing into their homes, into their food and their clothing?

What did they do in the night if they were ill and needed a doctor? In this township the size of a city where there were no hospitals? What did they do in the winter when it rained and that unforgiving wind still blew?

In the morning the wind had dropped. Mr Soyekwa greeted me warmly like a son and we ate breakfast together. Then a young woman called Bongiwe, who was a teacher, arrived to take us on a tour of the township in her car. The area was a mixture of basic housing, with running water and mains electricity – and shack dwellings with nothing. We saw corrugated iron shacks built on sand dunes with a shared hut latrine and a distant tap from which children would carry water in old plastic bottles. Occasionally we would stop and ask if we could see inside one of the dwellings. I half expected the people to be bitterly resentful of a rich tourist poking around in their private lives, but they were dignified and courteous.

Time after time we stopped; time after time I had the same surprise. Despite having no money and no resources, the homes were all spotlessly clean and tidy. Never did I catch the familiar smell of unclean living and nor did I see any litter. How they did it, I could not begin to understand. As we drove on I felt over-whelmed by the scale of the grotesque injustice which had been done to these people by a rich, white, Christian civilization. Mile after mile of social violence left me ashamed to have a white skin. Finally, I asked to go home. Back to Mr Soyekwa's house.

The next day was Sunday and I had been invited to preach at the local church of St Mary Magdalene. I do not know what I expected, but it was not a church of 800 people. During the service we sang old-fashioned Victorian hymns. There was a special collection for a family whose house had been burnt down in the night. Someone had died in the fire. There was deep sorrow and understanding. As I listened to the story of the fire, I suddenly realized what was being said. A fire among those crowded settlement dwellings? In that wind? With no fire engines? With no hose pipes?

A woman spontaneously started singing – not an old Victorian hymn, but an African song. Then something awesome happened. As the people came up to put money into the collection for the family, the deep and powerful music filled the church with a sound that seemed to embody the essence of the human spirit. I began to realize why these people had not died of despair or bitterness – and why, in their material poverty, they were queuing down the aisle in their hundreds to give what money they could to the survivors of the fire. For the first time in my life, I emptied the entire contents of my pockets onto a church collection plate.

Although the service was in the African language of Xhosa, with its strange clicking sounds, I could still follow the Eucharist from the booklet. As Mxolisi led us in the Lord's Prayer I realized we were all, in our different languages, saying the same words: Abba, dear Father. And in that moment I realized that these people who had shown me, a stranger, such love and generosity of spirit were my sisters and my brothers – and that, at the end of the service, I was going to have to leave them.

Two days before I had prayed desperately not to come to this place. Now I was praying I might be allowed to stay. More than anything in the world, I wanted to be Mxolisi's curate and stay in Guguletu.

Back in Cape Town, five hours later, I was taken to an open air jazz concert on a lush green hillside in the city's botanical gardens. Compared to Guguletu only a few miles down the road, it was a different world. But it was not my world. I felt alien and strange among the predominantly white people who sprawled on the grass listening to the music. What had happened? My centre of gravity had shifted. I was no longer at home in this old dispensation. I thought back to the arid coastal plain of Guguletu and the loving, prayerful people I had met there. I thought of the family whose home had been destroyed in the fire the previous night, and of the person who had died in that terrifying situation where there were no fire engines and no hospitals.

I thought about the singing and the Eucharist where 800 people had said in their own language Abba, dear Father. In that moment I had realized that prayer links people in a bond of love which you cannot then unfasten. Because it is an acknowledgement of reality.

—◆—

If we say the words Abba, dear Father, with our eyes open we are awestruck by the meaning of what is being uttered – that we should be permitted to address God as Father and to do so with the trusting familiarity of a child. And for a moment the realization we are loved by God dazzles us to the implications of that word.

To love God and to be loved by God is not an experience unique to me. It is for you also. But if we both share this life-giving experience, then what is our relationship to each other? And not only you and I, but also the other person – and all of us? And then we begin to understand the meaning and the source of Christ's commandment that we must love God with all our heart and our neighbour also. And who is our neighbour? Everyone is our neighbour because everyone is loved by God – we and they are enfolded in that love.

The trouble is that love means more than just warm feelings. To love means to seek the well-being of the other person and to work for that person's growth and fulfilment. It means opposing the injustice which damages that person and working alongside that person for the freedom to be themselves. It is only then that we begin to realize how politically dangerous the Lord's Prayer is – because many of the injustices which damage and degrade our neighbour are the consequences of our politics and economics. Even though people live on the other side of the world, they are our sisters and our brothers if we dare to say and mean the words, Abba, dear Father.

If we are all loved by God, then how can we not become involved in the struggle for justice and for peace among his children? At first that seems a totally alien and unacceptable suggestion. We are accustomed to religion being comforting, predictable and private. But if we say the first words of the Lord's Prayer, we suddenly discover that an encounter with the living God is none of those things – and that politics and economics are an essential part of prayer.

Day 7   Week 2

TUESDAY

THE THIRD-CLASS CHRIST

The town was buzzing with excitement. The remote rural community seldom received a visit from its bishop who was known to be a person of great holiness. But today he was coming to see them. Long before his train was due, the station was made ready with a ceremonial carpet and the band practised its welcoming music. As the great moment arrived the mayor and other civic dignitaries lined up on the platform. On time, the train slowly pulled in to the station and stopped with the first-class carriage exactly where the red carpet had been laid.

The mayor stepped forward and opened the first-class compartment door with a flourish. The carriage was empty. The band stopped playing. There was an embarrassed silence, broken only by laughter coming from further down the platform. Some people had emerged in high spirits from a second-class carriage. The mayor was annoyed, but then realized to his horror that among them was the missing bishop. Pushing through the crowd to get to their very important guest, the mayor said, 'Why on earth were you travelling in a second-class carriage?' The bishop answered with a smile, 'There was no third-class compartment on the train.'

—•—

Such mistakes and misunderstandings are amusing, as long as they happen to other people. But when they happen to us and it is we who are embarrassed, things are not so easily dealt with. And there is no doubt that, whether or not the bishop was in the wrong compartment, Jesus certainly was. And instead of ending with laughter, it ended with murder. But all that is weeks away. For now let us explore how it all started to go wrong. In chapter 7 of his gospel, St Luke describes a series of dramatic events – and at each stage the voltage is stepped up until we reach a point where the tension becomes almost unbearable.

The first event is the healing of a slave owned by a Roman centurion, and the way it comes about is extraordinary. First of all, the centurion sends a message to Jesus asking him to come and heal his slave who is dangerously ill. But, after his friends have left to find Jesus, the centurion suddenly realizes something important about this Jewish preacher. To the astonishment of his other servants, he sends a further message. The second message is astounding. He tells Jesus not to bother coming to his house, but simply to speak the word of healing. The centurion is an army officer, vested with authority. In his anxious vigil at the bedside of the dying slave, the centurion has suddenly realized that Jesus is also a person vested with authority. 'Do not trouble yourself to come; simply give the order,' says the soldier. Jesus gives the word and, says Luke, at that moment the slave is healed.

The audacity of the man's faith is clear, for Jesus himself says, 'Never in the whole nation of God's people have I seen such faith.' His highest praise is spoken for a pagan soldier in a foreign army. Luke's story has not just been about healing, but about the power and authority of Jesus – and the exercise of that power and authority outside the confines of the Jewish community of faith. The centurion was not Jewish.

But now Luke takes us a stage further and the tension rises perceptibly. Jesus is walking with his followers towards a town called Nain. Coming the other way is a funeral procession, accompanied by a great crowd of mourners. The death has been particularly tragic – a young man has died and he was the only son of his widowed mother. Robbed, first of her husband, and now her only son, the woman is distraught with grief. What happens next is amazing.

Instead of stepping respectfully aside to let the body pass by, Jesus halts the funeral. Moved with a deep compassion he puts his hand on the open coffin. He speaks words of loving reassurance to the heartbroken mother and, to everyone's amazement, raises the dead boy to life. The crowd are stunned until someone says the words which may well cost Jesus his own life: 'God has visited his people.'

What has happened here is as shocking as it is surprising. First, this man of God breaks the law of God. In a gesture of loving concern he touches the open coffin – and in doing so he is ritually defiled. But he has no need to touch the coffin. Second, he concerns himself with a group of total strangers. He has no need to get involved. Unlike the centurion, whose faith was deeper than any Jesus has seen in the whole nation, he raises the dead child to life without asking for a single word of faith from the grieving mother.

Luke is showing a greater act of power and authority by Jesus, but at the same time revealing that love to be operative without our asking – and regardless of the religious laws which we have created. 'God has visited his people' shouts someone in the crowd with an inspired lack of good sense. They are right. But what sort of God is it that is moved with a deep love at the sight of suffering, unnecessarily breaks the religious law and restores life to a total stranger?

It is certainly not the sort of God that either the religious leaders, or John the Baptist, were hoping and praying would intervene to rescue the nation from its troubles. And Luke recognizes this. There is a rising tension in the story as John's disciples report back to their own leader. John is being held in prison and is in danger of his life. What is going on out there? He has baptized Jesus in the

Jordan after telling the crowds that this is the one who will come bringing violent retribution – the Messiah John has been proclaiming is a warrior leader, a man of the sword. Suddenly John is confused and alarmed: Who is this person?

He dispatches some of his disciples to ask Jesus who he is. They find Jesus among the outcasts and the sick. 'Are you the one who is to come or are we to look for another person?' they ask. Jesus does not answer their question directly. Instead he tells them, 'Go and tell John what you see. The blind receive their sight and the lame walk again. The lepers are healed and the good news of life is spoken to the poor.' And then Jesus adds a word of loving assurance for his friend in prison: Blessed is the one who does not find me a stumbling block. I may not have been in the compartment you expected and what you hear may be difficult for you to understand and grasp. But blessed are you if you can grasp this truth about the power and the love of God. We are in an 'Abba' situation. It has caught John unawares and, in his confusion and despair, Jesus speaks a word of brotherly encouragement.

John's disciples leave to report back to their leader. But Jesus has not finished. The tension is about to reach breaking point. Turning to the crowds, Jesus challenges them: What did you all go out to the Jordan to see? Because, whatever it was you hoped for, I tell you no greater person ever walked the earth. John was the culmination of the greatest people in our history – the prophet Elijah and the lawgiver, Moses. And what has happened to this great person? You have locked him up in prison.

Then Jesus launches into a powerful attack on the people and on the religious authorities. What are you like? he says angrily. You are like a bunch of spoilt and spiteful kids. John came living a life of godly simplicity and eating a meagre diet of the most basic food, and you condemned him as being mad. Now, says Jesus, I come eating and drinking with anyone and everyone and you call me a glutton and a drunkard, a friend of tax collectors and sinners. But be warned, says Jesus, God's will is going to prevail.

The danger of the situation and the tension it creates arise not because of the unexpected nature of what is happening, but because of vested interests. Sometimes these vested interests are simply the emotional assumptions of the people: we have always done things this way – do not try to change things, we are comfortable with things the way they are.

–•–

But sometimes the explosion comes because of the vested interests of the powerful. Meeting the bishop's train at the station, the mayor found himself in an embarrassing situation. The assembled civic leaders, the band and the red carpet were all in the wrong place; or the bishop was in the wrong carriage. But the bishop was in the right carriage – it was just not the first-class one they had expected. The bishop was a second-class bishop and that was what made him holy. It was the nearest he could get to the third-class Christ he followed.

The mayor was prepared to walk down the platform; to meet the bishop halfway and to share in the laughter. But for Jesus, the religious leaders and civic dignitaries waiting for him were to be less forgiving.

–•–

Day 8   Week 2
WEDNESDAY
THE FIRST EXPLOSION

It is a sure sign of advancing years when you disapprove of the behaviour of young people while ignoring the fact that you were just like that yourself as a child. Like the times we used to put fireworks in metal dustbins and wait for the bang. This worked particularly well if the dustbin was empty – but you had to remember to put the lid on after you had dropped the firework inside. The lid makes for a better bang.

What is true in this trivial example of childhood delinquency is also true in the much more serious matter of human relationships.

It is no coincidence that a large proportion of acts of violence and murder take place within the confines of the family. While traditionalists extol the virtues of family life, they are less willing to acknowledge the fact that families are often places of violence and suffering. This may be partly due to the fact that when we ourselves are in pain we often hit out at the people nearest to us; but it may also be to do with the fact that the traditional family is an enclosed unit – rather like the dustbin with the lid on it.

And what happens in families can also happen in communities. Reading the story of how Christ's ministry began, we begin to realize how close he came to never having a ministry at all. Luke describes an incident in which Jesus so angers a group of people that they try to murder him. And the people he angers are his own townspeople – his own neighbours in Nazareth where he was brought up. The story is fascinating because it is an example of how energy in a confined space often leads to an explosion.

—•—

Jesus, after his baptism and the time of temptation in the desert, returns to Galilee, the region where he had been brought up. But this is not a casual visit. He is returning 'in the power of the Spirit' – full of purpose and conviction and driven by the compelling power of God. He goes to the synagogue on the Sabbath and is invited to read from the scriptures. He finds the passage from Isaiah:

> The Spirit of the Lord is upon me because he has anointed me to bring the Good News to the poor. To proclaim release for the prisoners and recovery of sight for the blind; to let the broken victims go free and to proclaim the year of the Lord's favour.

When he finishes reading, Jesus says to the assembled people, 'Today, at this moment, in your very hearing, this has come true.' It takes a few moments for the impact of that statement to sink in and, while it is doing so, maybe we could explore a few of the things that are happening.

First, Jesus is claiming that what he is doing is with the authority of God. He is saying that what is to follow is to be carried out as God's agenda, as an expression of the will and nature of God. Monarchs are anointed at their coronation as a sign of empowerment and commissioning. Jesus is saying he is commissioned by God to fulfil the task he is about to describe.

Second, his appointed task has an overall summary statement. It is the Isaiah reading he has chosen – to proclaim good news to the poor. The word for poor is the word Luke also uses in the Beatitudes: 'Blessed are the poor.' But unlike Matthew's gospel which softens the meaning to read 'poor in spirit', Luke means the physically destitute – the beggars. He is resolute. He does not simply mean spiritual poverty.

Third, as he goes through his agenda, Jesus says his God-given task is to express love and acceptance for exactly those people whom the religious establishment believed were excluded from God's love. One of the reasons John the Baptist had been so confused by Jesus was because he welcomed and accepted the very people John expected him to condemn. These riff-raff would be destroyed in an outpouring of the wrath of God, he had warned.

Meanwhile, the congregation in the synagogue are just beginning to realize something else Jesus has said. That it is he, the son of a local carpenter, who is to be the agent by which the will of God is to be worked out. Gradually the mood of admiration for the local boy is changing to indignation and fury.

Then Jesus drops the final bombshell. The good news, he says, is not just for the Jews. Contrary to other parts of the gospels where Jesus indicates he has come first and foremost for the sake of his own nation, here is a clear signal that the good news of God's life-giving love is for all people. For any who will accept it. The tragedy is that these people, his friends and neighbours, will not accept him. Nor, in the years to come, will his own faith community be able to contain him. As St John says in the majestic opening words of the Fourth Gospel: 'His own would not receive him.'

And in the next few moments, the congregation in the synagogue are going to give concrete expression to that rejection. This person is too close for comfort. In the enclosed space of the synagogue – and in the enclosed space of the community in which Jesus has been brought up – there is no room to accommodate such revolutionary and heretical teaching.

Like a body which has swallowed something indigestible, they vomit out this person from the synagogue – hurling him out of the building and dragging him to a cliff from which they propose to throw him to his death.

There is seemingly no space for them to explore coolly and objectively what is being said. The issue is not whether this person is right or wrong, sane or mad; it is simply that they cannot cope with the voltage which he is generating. He will bring disgrace on their synagogue with his heretical teachings and claims – and he will bring disgrace on the community in which he has been brought up.

––◆––

What we are talking about here is the dynamics of change. Energy released in an enclosed space is what makes a car move, but energy released can also create damaging explosions. The basic problem which Jesus revealed is that God is by nature energy for change. From the first words of the creation saga of the Old Testament we have known it – God is the creative force which brings life into being. The Spirit of God is pictured in the book of Genesis hovering over the waters of chaos in that first primeval act of creation. The problem arises when human beings want to enclose and control that creative force. If we try to shut that energy up in a box or a metal dustbin, we are likely to end up with a loud bang.

But religious people do not like loud bangs. The whole ethos of the Church is one of quietness and solemnity; stability and predictability. Our church buildings are the essence of stability and silence. We talk about 'finding our rest in God' and, in the old Prayer Book, asking that we may be 'godly and quietly governed'. Perhaps we need to examine the possibility that God may not be quiet and docile – and that the Christ person may be a very challenging and provocative figure.

Energy bursting out of confined spaces seems at first sight to have little to do with life. But how else does a butterfly get out of a chrysalis – or a baby from the womb? In his explosive sermon to the congregation in the synagogue, Jesus was saying that it was

time to break free from the confined space of their religious structures. And he may be saying the same thing to us this Lent.

───◄●►───

Day 9   Week 2
THURSDAY
THE LAUGHTER OF GOD

We read so many newspapers in Britain, there is a danger we may
start to believe some of the things they say. However, to take just
two examples: the inner city is not as dangerous as they say it is;
and nuns are not as boring as you might think.

One day a friend who is an Anglican sister had a frightening
experience. She was walking to the shops when she suddenly
heard the sound of running feet. Turning round she saw an Asian
youth racing towards her. Thinking she was about to be mugged,
she clutched her bag tightly to her body. But as he ran past, the
youth grinned broadly. 'Prayers, sister,' he said. 'Late for prayers!'

Later she reflected she could not remember having seen anyone, of whatever age or colour, running to say their prayers in
church. And if they did – would they be laughing about it? In
fact, are Christians typified by their sense of fun and enjoyment of
life – a sense of exuberance? The answer is they are not.

But what about Jesus? What sort of a character was he? The
process of religious containment which has gone on over the last
two thousand years, not least in the imagery in paintings and
stained glass windows, has produced a Christ figure which is safe
and sanitized – and unbearably dull. The question we need to ask
is whether that image is true to life.

Reading the source documents of the Christian faith is rather
like reading the script of a play. We hear the words, but we do not
engage with the drama of the situation. It takes a significant act of
will to allow our imagination to open the scriptures up to us.

During a recent visit to South Africa, I was having a meal with a group of people, one of whom was a devout Christian. He had recently taken part in a major church training event and was full of enthusiasm for what he had discovered. It seemed, however, he was not planning to stay in South Africa. Instead he was emigrating to Australia. Did he have friends there, I asked. No, he knew no one there. Had he a job to go to? No, but he would find one. Why was he going to Australia then, I asked. The blacks, he said. The blacks? Yes – since the end of apartheid the blacks were taking over in South Africa and he had to get out.

I thought for a minute about whether it was worth suggesting that it *was* their country – or that the black people I knew were light years ahead of him in human development. Instead I said, 'What colour do you think Jesus was?' There was a moment's hesitation then, 'White, of course,' he said.

In one sense it does not matter whether Jesus was white, black or green, but just for the record he was probably much the same colour as the Asian youth who gave my friend the nun a bit of a fright. Not only was he probably a deep shade of brown, but he was certainly young. And it may even be that just occasionally he ran down the street and laughed.

Think for a moment about some of the events described in the gospels – and ask yourself how this young 30-year-old might have behaved. Even in moments of sadness and anger, the laughter is visible. Speaking about the way John the Baptist has been rejected and then imprisoned, Jesus describes with a loving familiarity the parallel course which the two of them have followed for a time. He ate little and lived simply and you said he was crazy, says Jesus. I eat and drink with the gang and you call me a glutton and a drunkard.

I suspect Jesus was probably not a glutton or a drunkard, but just as there may have been a grain of truth in the picture of John's grim austerity, perhaps there may also have been a truth in the way Jesus is described. Does someone who is criticized for being a glutton and drunkard not sometimes enjoy food and wine? Did he eat and drink in holy silence? Did he not occasionally laugh with others in the good company of a big meal? When he coaxed Zacchaeus down out of the sycamore tree and told the swindling tax collector he was inviting himself round for supper, was there no laughter? When Zacchaeus reacted by confessing his faults and in a spontaneous act of reparation offered to give back several times over what he had taken, did Jesus not hug him with delight?

Jesus even portrays the love of God in a wonderfully undignified way. Remember the story of the prodigal son? The father in that story is Christ's picture of God. The son goes off with his share of the inheritance leaving his father deeply concerned for the boy's safety. Each day the father scans the horizon for a sign of the son's return. Then at last he sees him, far off in the distance. But what does the father do? Wait patiently for the son to reach the farm gate? No, says Jesus, the father hitches up his robes and runs down the dusty road to meet him and, even though the boy is covered in filth, he flings his arms round him in a joyful, tearful embrace. And was there no laughter?

Even in St John's great gospel, which is far less earthy than the others, there are situations where the laughter of Jesus can be heard. And if the laughter of Christ, then why not the laughter of God, if this is the human form of God?

Think about that strange story of the wedding at Cana in Galilee. Year in and year out the story is read in church. And no one laughs. Why? Because they are not hearing what is said. Perhaps because they do not want to hear what is being said. And they are not using their imagination.

According to the story Jesus goes to a wedding but, to the deep embarrassment of the host, they run out of wine. There are some huge storage jars each with a capacity of 20 to 30 gallons. 'Fill them with water,' says Jesus. The servants fill them to the brim. Then Jesus tells them to draw some of the water off and take it to the steward. The water has turned into wine, says John.

But why should anyone laugh? Because Jesus has just done something wonderfully outrageous, according to St John. He has just produced about 150 gallons of wine. That is enough wine not just for the wedding but for the entire population of the village.

They have enough wine to bath in. There is more wine than they have ever seen before. One moment they are without wine and plunged into the degrading humiliation felt often by the poor – that they do not have the material resources to express their own generosity. But the next minute they are flooded out with the stuff. It is as though they have suddenly gone from death to resurrection. They are given back their rightful dignity, as well as wine. Freed from the imprisonment of poverty – restored to life. Life by the gallon. And was there no laughter?

Perhaps St John did not mean it to be taken that way. Perhaps the storage jars were not so big. Perhaps Jesus said just fill the one – not all six. Perhaps we do not like to think of the Son of God as the sort of person who laughs or drinks or enjoys food – or enjoys life. The one who said he had come that we might have life in all its fullness.

Maybe we just want to create Christ in our own narrow image, and justify the way we are by the person we imagine him to have been. The trouble is, when we read the gospels, we meet a different person from the one we see in the stained glass windows of churches where you must not laugh or make a noise.

Maybe that is why you do not often see joyful people running to church to pray.

———◆———

Day 10   Week 2

FRIDAY

THE DANGER OF DRAINPIPES

A recent survey of church people came up with a very amusing result. The people taking part in the opinion poll were asked to list the things they thought the Church should be doing – what God was asking it to do in the world. They were then asked to rank these tasks in order of importance. They were also asked to say what things they thought the Church was best at doing – and, again, to list these in order of success or achievement.

The result of the survey was that church people said the primary task of the Church was to live out the love of Christ in the world. The job that came bottom of the list, as least important, they said, was looking after church buildings. However, when it came to listing the things the Church actually did best in real life, the result was just the opposite: top of the list came church buildings – and bottom of the list came living out God's love in the world.

Amusing it was, but surprising it should not have been. After all, it is a lot easier to paint a drainpipe than it is to start putting the Gospel into practice. And for many people, their local church building is not only a place of worship, it is also a major source of emotional security – a visible sign of stability in a changing world. But buildings cost money and if we do not look after our gutters and drainpipes, we are going to have financial problems.

Little wonder that our church buildings are probably in better shape than they have ever been, even though fewer people than ever actually go to church. Thanks to the attention of people like English Heritage, the Victorian Society, diocesan surveyors and architects as well as church wardens and archdeacons, who all have a particular responsibility for church fabric, this is the day of the drainpipe.

But drainpipes can be dangerous. Not the ones the water comes down – but the ones our prayers go up. Or have you never realized that many people pray up a drainpipe? They pray as though they have a personal line to God and what is said is a private matter between the two of them. You can often recognize people with a drainpipe faith when they start talking about Jesus as 'my' Lord and Saviour. About their relationship with God as 'my' personal faith. There is a narrow tube of communication up which the prayers go.

The Church often prays up drainpipes. For example, there is still a widely held view that spiritual matters must be kept separate from worldly matters, as though God needed protecting from the world he has created. This narrow 'drainpipe theology' is not a new thing – it has its origins far back, 3,500 years ago in the earliest days of the Hebrew people. They saw themselves as being set apart from the world – as chosen people.

—•—

When they invaded the territory of Canaan, believing it to be the land promised to them by God, they believed it was essential to keep themselves separate from the indigenous people. For many years they co-existed in an uneasy peace, but there was a problem. Things were getting too friendly.

Being the newcomers to Canaan, the Hebrews lived in the less fertile hills where, for the most part, they kept cattle and sheep. But, having arrived first and chosen the prime site, down on the rich coastal plain, the Canaanites grew crops. And each community was influenced in its understanding of God by its environment.

The Hebrews believed their God had led them on a great trek to this promised land and all they had was the Lord's. Meanwhile, down on the lowland plains, the Canaanites were deeply aware of their dependence on their gods for the fertility of the land. Without that fertility there would be no crops and, not surprisingly, they envisaged their gods as being in a relationship of procreation with the earth. It was a theology which affirmed the life-giving gift of sexuality and the importance of their gods' participation in that process.

The problem was that friendly relationships began to develop between the Hebrews on the hills and the Canaanites on the lowland plains. There is archaeological evidence that many people worshipped the God of the Hebrews and the deities of the Canaanites at the same time. As is often the case with minority immigrant groups, this began to threaten the social and religious identity of the Hebrews. And to compromise their allegiance to God.

It is difficult to know which came first, but there seems little doubt that, while the system of worship which the Hebrews developed was primarily intended to give honour to God, it also served to distinguish them from their Canaanite neighbours. Over the years the Hebrews built up an elaborate pattern of ritual law and practice which set them apart. This involved the sacrifice of bulls, sheep and goats – and a need for ritual cleanliness and separation from the tribal group on the plains below.

The rituals seem strange to us now – animals had to be slaughtered in a certain way and the blood thrown against the altar. Parts of the animal were to be offered to God by being burnt while others could be eaten. Some foods were forbidden including pork, crab and lobster, as were homosexual relationships. All were an abomination – which meant to be avoided. Work on the seventh day of the week, the Sabbath, including even the lighting of a fire in your home, was forbidden and was technically punishable by death. Women were deemed to be unclean during their monthly periods of menstruation – as were those who had recently given birth.

Whether it was intentional or not, in their attempt to honour God and to keep themselves separate from the Canaanite host community, the Hebrews were constructing a theological drainpipe.

–◆–

This drainpipe mentality of purity and segregation was to cause huge problems for Jesus 1,500 years later. Time after time in the gospels we see Jesus breaking this inherited religious code of behaviour – and being attacked by the authorities for doing so. His disciples did not wash their hands before eating food; he himself worked on the Sabbath; he sat and shared food and fellowship with unclean sinners. He even claimed these sinners would be welcomed into heaven by God, while many of the narrowly religious people would be excluded.

It was this collision with the narrow restrictiveness of the religious establishment which ultimately sent Jesus to the cross. He would not accept their drainpipe.

The problem for us is that, after the death of Christ and the birth of the Church, the drainpipe effect began to happen again. Whereas the relationships which Jesus had engaged in with tax collectors, prostitutes and sinners were typically open and inclusive, after the first few years of the early Church the barriers begin to be re-erected.

The Church has historically seen itself as separate from the world – an exclusive group destined for salvation. Entry into the fellowship of Christ in first-century Palestine had been as easy as walking into a pub or climbing down out of a sycamore tree. But entry into the Church was different. There was a formal process of initiation into this exclusive group, which began to call itself the Body of Christ and to claim for itself chosen-people status.

─◆─

Nor are the damaging effects of this drainpipe theology a thing of the past. The idea of an exclusive and chosen people with a private line to God has had some of its most catastrophic consequences in the apartheid system in South Africa. This system depended in large part for its success on the view that the Afrikaaners, and other white Christian groups, were chosen people destined by God to possess the land. And entitled to enslave or exterminate the indigenous black population in the process.

The attraction of drainpipe theology is obvious – it gives a sense of security. But it is false security, as many white people in South Africa have begun to realize. Not only that, it is also spiritually false because it denies the essential nature of God. As we have seen, the Lord's Prayer begins with the words: 'Abba, dearest Father'. But 'Abba' is not a drainpipe word. It is a word which says that all of creation, black and white, Canaanite and Hebrew, is held in the loving hand of God and that each of us is sister and brother to the other.

It says the determining rule in our relationships with each other should be a love which reflects the life-giving love of God. Drainpipes are useful for preserving buildings but they do not make very good channels for love.

Day 11   Week 2
SATURDAY
WHO IS MY BROTHER?

It is no wonder that fewer people go to the theatre than go to the cinema. Films are simple; plays are often more complicated. At least with a film you know where you are. First the lights go out and the curtains open. Then there are the adverts and the trailers for new films. Then the main picture starts. And you sit in your seat and watch. At the end the credits roll, the curtains close and you go home. Easy.

But the last time I went to a play it was not easy. For a start, I did not know whether I was in the play or the audience. Second, the principal actor did not say a word throughout the entire show.

Or was it a show? The play was the drama-documentary of the Stephen Lawrence inquiry, *The Colour of Justice*. The action took place in a courtroom and was a dramatized re-enactment of the inquiry into how a young black student had been stabbed to death in a racist attack in London. The police had been accused of incompetence in their murder investigation, but the far more serious implications were that they had been both corrupt and racist. It was alleged they had colluded with known criminals who had links with Stephen's attackers – and had been indifferent to a successful outcome to the investigation because Stephen was black.

During the play a series of witnesses were called and questioned about the events leading up to the young man's death. A moving statement was read out from Stephen's friend who was with him when he was attacked. He was bitterly critical of the police who, he said, had done nothing to save Stephen's life.

But during the whole performance one person sat silent and motionless on the stage – Stephen's father. At first I thought it must have been easy for that actor to walk on stage, sit for three hours saying nothing and then walk off. But on reflection I suspect it was very hard work. In fact the actor gave an amazingly eloquent performance. He did not speak any words, but his expression of profound grief and his body language as he sat listening, over and over again, to the different versions of how his son had been murdered was amazingly powerful.

As the inquiry proceeded, it was impossible not to feel an increasing sense of involvement in what was going on, and a rising sense of anger at the injustice which had taken place – not just in the murder of Stephen Lawrence, but also in the degrading treatment his family had received. In response to all that, the silence of the father spoke more clearly than any words about the pain which was being experienced – as well as the awesome dignity with which it was being borne.

Then, at the end of the play, something very odd happened. The chairman of the tribunal asked everyone in the court to stand for a minute's silence in Stephen's memory – and he asked the audience to stand as well. We all stood in silence. And the effect was devastating.

But were we in the play or outside it? And was it a play at all? The powerful effect of the drama was partly due to the fact that it was a true story which everyone in the audience was familiar with and felt deeply about. But the effect was also powerful because the play crossed the line between actors and audience. They were playing a real-life drama and we, the audience, were part of that drama.

Years ago, when people were ordained, it was said they had 'gone into' the Church, rather as they might have 'gone into' the Army or the Navy. Whatever it was they had gone into, it was something different. It was not ordinary life.

But how strange that is when you remember the whole point of the birth of Christ, what the Church calls the Incarnation, was exactly the opposite of that. It was God being deeply involved in ordinary life. Born as a human being and working at an ordinary trade, the Christ person was nothing less than God present in the ordinary stuff of the everyday world. No drainpipe.

And perhaps that was what was so powerfully effective about the play – no curtain; no drainpipe. Even though I am not black and I have never had anyone close to me die violently, I was able to identify very strongly with the father in the drama. Partly perhaps because I am a father and I had a sense of what the real father of Stephen Lawrence must have felt. But I was also deeply moved because the father reminded me of God.

Whether it was the expression on the actor's face or his grief-stricken silence, I am not sure, but it was as though he was God looking with mute sorrow on the pain and violence of the world. There was a moment in the drama when we were told how Stephen had said good-bye to his father, minutes before he left the house on the night on which he was murdered, and I wondered in the darkness of the theatre what word he had used in that parting moment. Was it Dad? Was it Daddy? Was it Abba? No, of course not. An ordinary teenager living in London is not likely to speak to his Dad in first-century Aramaic. And yet I suspect the word he used translated 'Abba' exactly.

I thought about the words of St John's Gospel where the writer describes God allowing his only Son to be born into the world – and how he must have known what would happen. I thought about the father looking out of the window month after month for a glimpse of his prodigal son's return, dreading the news that he had been murdered in some far-off place.

I thought back to what Jesus said when he was told his mother, brothers and sisters were at the door. He said his real mother and brothers and sisters are those who do the will of God. He, too, was crossing boundaries.

Coming out of the theatre I wondered who this Stephen Lawrence was, because it felt as though he was my son, too, and that the pain was mine as well. There had been no curtains on the stage. The boundaries had not been clear. If God is Father to us all and we are held in that life-breathing love, then there can be no boundaries. No black, no white. No drainpipes.

Day 12   Week 3
SECOND SUNDAY OF LENT
Driving Force

Small boys can be disgusting little creatures. I was one. What they get up to these days, other than play video games, I am not sure, but we were little monsters when we were young. One of our objectionable activities was to make bows and arrows. Tearing the smaller branches off trees and using the string always to be found in small boys' pockets, we would construct the bow. Small branches would then be cannibalized to make the arrows. Whether we ever hit anything, I cannot remember – fortunately no one ever sustained serious injury.

Our inspiration was the enthralling story of the Battle of Agincourt and the legendary power of the English long-bow. This was such a powerful weapon it could operate at a range far beyond the reach of enemy fire and propel arrows with such force they could punch holes in body armour at great distances. In an age of high technology, we assume bows and arrows are a thing of the past, but the principle they operate on is still very much with us.

―•―

A naval officer was once in trouble for the misuse of the hydraulic catapult on his ship. The catapult was designed to launch a light aircraft from the vessel while the ship was at sea. He, however, had used it to launch his elderly Austin Seven car. It was one of the most spectacular examples of a burial at sea; and certainly the fastest journey ever made by an Austin Seven. The ship's catapult operated on the same principle as the bow and arrow. The projectile is placed in the firing apparatus; the cable which will launch the projectile is drawn back, building up huge potential energy, before being released – driving the missile forward at great speed. An athlete throwing a javelin or a baseball player pitching a ball operates in the same way – the arm is drawn back and then flung forward as the ball or javelin is thrown.

―•―

It may sound surprising, but that is exactly what happens in the Lord's Prayer. We are often led to think of Jesus as a passive person, telling stories and healing people in quiet serenity, but seldom getting into a sweat. But perhaps in our exploration of the Lord's Prayer, we might think of him more as an athlete – or as an archer shooting an arrow from a bow.

Think for a moment what is happening when Jesus teaches his disciples the Lord's Prayer. They have come to him and found him praying. When he finishes, they say to him: 'Teach us to pray, as John taught his disciples.' We need to be clear that they are not asking him to show them how to pray – every Jew knew how to pray. What they are asking is that Jesus will teach them *his* way of praying, just as John the Baptist taught his disciples how he prayed.

Teach us your way of praying, they say. Jesus does as they ask, but it is not a passive recital of words. It is as though Jesus stoops and picks up a powerful bow. Then he fits a most amazing arrow to the string. He draws back the arrow, bending the powerful bow until the string is against his face. Both muscle and bow are now flexed and at full tension, ready to drive the arrow of prayer forward in an explosive release of energy.

And that is exactly the point we have arrived at today in the Lord's Prayer. Teach us to pray your way, they ask him. Help us to reach our target of speaking to God and listening to his word. And he does. But they are not prepared for what happens next.

Jesus picks up the arrow, but it is one they have never seen before. It is the word 'Abba'. Used in its normal domestic context, it is a gentle word. But in the hands of Jesus it is powerful. It is a word of trust such as a child would use for a parent, but it carries with it an awesome authority. We are about to address Almighty God with the familiar loving word which we can translate as 'dearest Father' – and we have hardly begun to work out the implications of what we are saying.

Jesus fits the arrow to the bow and then does what every archer does – he draws back his arm and, in doing so, develops increasing power. But he draws back his arm in the second line of the Lord's Prayer by suddenly and unexpectedly pulling us back, deep into the spiritual tradition of his people. The second line of the Lord's

Prayer, 'hallowed be thy name', is an expression steeped in Hebrew history.

It is from an ancient Aramaic prayer called the *kaddish* which is used regularly in the worship of the synagogue. The prayer reads: 'exalted and hallowed be thy great name.'

The 'name' of God was not simply an identifying label. In fact the Hebrew tradition avoided using the name of God, preferring instead to use the expression 'the Lord'. What was signified by the name was nothing less than the presence and authority of God. The place where the Lord makes his name to dwell is the place where God's presence is to be experienced. God is there.

Just as it is about the presence of God, so it is also about the power and authority of God. We are familiar with stories in which a messenger will convey a command in the name of the king, or a police officer will make an arrest in the name of the law. How strange that this idea of the name of the Lord is a constant refrain in the writings of the Old Testament. Yet we hear it on the lips of Jesus only once. Here in the Lord's Prayer.

Second, it could be said that to hallow the name of God was the basic motivation of the Hebrew faith. Why else did they exist but to show honour and reverence to the presence and authority of God? Their whole lives were to be dedicated to that end and, from earliest childhood, every person in the community would have been familiar with that duty and privilege.

So what is happening? Jesus tells them how to pray, first, by presenting them with the revolutionary Abba concept, never before used in prayer by the community of faith. Never used by his God-centred community, but always used in prayer by Jesus. That is the contrast of what was now happening and what had gone before. But now, in one short sentence, Jesus draws them suddenly back into their spiritual heritage – back to the worship of the synagogue. Grounding what is to come in the tradition of the community.

And that process sounds strangely familiar. St Mark does exactly the same thing in the opening words of his terse and abrasive gospel. There he begins with the equally revolutionary concept that Jesus, the Christ, is the Good News. 'Here begins the Good News of Jesus Christ.' The Good News is not news about Jesus, it is Jesus himself. But then Mark does a remarkable thing – having made his revolutionary opening statement, he too immediately pulls us back, deep into the spiritual tradition of the community with the words: 'In the prophet Isaiah it stands written . . .'

The same powerful dynamic is operating. The arrow is fitted and then drawn back, flexing the bow and increasing the driving force. With Mark it is the powerful words of the first gospel ever written. With Jesus it is something even more explosive.

Day 13   Week 3

MONDAY

DOES HE TAKE SUGAR?

One of my most embarrassing moments occurred when I was watching television one day. There appeared on the screen a man in a wheelchair. His body and face were twisted out of shape and it was clear after a few seconds he was unable to speak. Assuming he was in some way brain-damaged and not much wanting to be confronted with this grossly disfigured person, I reached to change TV channels.

It was only then I realized that the man in the wheelchair was Stephen Hawking, professor of mathematics at Cambridge University and famous for his work on theoretical physics and, in particular, for his research on the origins of the universe. Far from being brain-damaged, he has been described as one of the most brilliant minds since Einstein.

Hawking says he was 'unlucky enough' to get motor neurone disease. Some years later he lost the ability to speak after catching pneumonia and having a tracheostomy operation. He now communicates using a synthesizer and personal computer mounted on his wheelchair. He is still doing his research into theoretical physics which is extending our knowledge of the universe. Meanwhile I am still trying to read his book, *A Brief History of Time,* and to forgive myself for assuming that a person in a wheelchair who was unable to speak, did not have either human dignity or a brain. Rather like the man offering a blind person a cup of tea who asked the woman sitting with him: Does he take sugar?

—◆—

As we have seen, when we say the words 'hallowed be thy name' in the Lord's Prayer we are recognizing and honouring the personhood and authority of God. We are showing reverence for the presence of God himself. Translating that into another of the sayings Jesus used, we could say we are loving God with all our mind and heart and strength.

But maybe, when we begin to do this, we should also try to hallow each other's name, so that we reverence and honour other people. Perhaps this is to do with the second part of the great commandment of Jesus – that we love our neighbour. Loving our neighbour involves recognizing the reality of the person before us, and not allowing appearances to deceive us. The person in a wheelchair is there because their legs, and maybe other parts, don't work well enough for them to stand up and walk. Being in a wheelchair does not say anything about what else that person may be able to do. The same applies to any other characteristic, whether it is age, skin colour, gender or sexual orientation.

Happily, Stephen Hawking has many people across the world who hallow his name, partly by their respect for his courage and his scientific achievements, but also for the person he is. His sense of humour and his humility. In 'hallowing his name' in that way, they are in fact loving him. And if they are loving him, then what is God doing?

Perhaps God is also loving Stephen Hawking and hallowing his name. At first that may sound a ridiculous idea. We began exploring the meaning of the Lord's Prayer – our prayer to God – and before we are past the second sentence here we are thinking about the process happening in reverse. How can we say that God might be hallowing our name?

It is when we ask this question that we begin to hear echoes from one of the great writings of the Old Testament – the same spiritual tradition which was rooted in the idea of hallowing God's name. There, in the writings of Isaiah, we hear the words:

> Fear not, for I have redeemed you.
> I have called you by name and you
> are mine . . .
> I am your God . . . your saviour.
> You are precious in my eyes and honoured
> And I love you.

These words were written by Isaiah as a proclamation of reassurance to his fellow captives in exile. God is pictured as saying to the Hebrews that, even in their captivity, he is speaking words of freedom and release. To be redeemed means to be liberated from the slavery of debt, while to be called by name indicates a direct and focused relationship between two people.

Then comes one of the most powerful statements in the whole Bible: 'You [a group of impoverished captives existing, apparently forgotten, in some foreign land] are precious in my eyes. You are honoured and I love you.' It is a great cry of hope and exultation; of an overarching faith in God, the Almighty One. A faith which says that with him all things are possible.

It is a cry of exultation which is echoed 500 years later by someone not held in captivity or in a wheelchair, but a woman – and therefore someone of equally little account. She, too, is called by name and hallowed by God. And, in the words of the *Magnificat*, Mary speaks as powerfully as Isaiah all those centuries before in her own statement of freedom and liberation:

> My soul magnifies the Lord because he has regarded [hallowed] his lowly servant. From henceforth all nations will count me blessed [hallow me] . . . For he has put down the mighty from their thrones and the humble have been lifted up. He has filled the hungry with good things – and the rich he has sent away empty.

As we hallow God's name, so too God loves and hallows us. It is the love of God which calls forth our response and draws us into life. Who knows, it could even be this love which is the origin of the universe.

———◄●►———

Day 14   Week 3
TUESDAY
THE TIGHTROPE WALKER

Eve rang last night. She was in tears. She has a terrible cold and she is desperately unhappy. She says she has made a big mistake coming to theological college. A week into her two-year course she wants to go home. I tell her to take some paracetamol, have lots of hot drinks and get plenty of sleep. She does not want to sleep, she wants to pack. The other students training for ordination are different from her. 'I don't fit in here,' she says. I think about her long, red-painted finger nails, her black leather trousers and her blonde hair and I know what she means. Both she and the college are on a steep learning curve. I hold my breath and pray that God will keep the miracle alive. Has she come this far for it all to end in failure?

Eve is a long way from home, feeling isolated and afraid. Walking a tightrope, she faces two dangers. One is that she will quit or be asked to leave by a college which does not quite have the courage of its convictions. The other danger is even worse – it is that they will change her, moulding her into a middle-class religious clone instead of remaining the dynamic, wonderful, Christ-centred person she is now.

Over the phone I try to think of the words which have been going round in my head for the last few days: 'Fear not, for I have redeemed you. I am your God, your saviour. You are precious in my eyes' ('Just as you are, beloved child, with your red nail varnish and your leather trousers. Even though you still haven't given up smoking.') 'You are honoured and I love you.'

Suddenly the words of Isaiah are the most powerful ever written.

I hang up and I, too, am in tears. What is going on? Why does it matter so much? Because the Gospel is happening before our very eyes. This young woman who has been called whore and hooker and slapper and tart is now being called by God. And what is God saying?

'I have called you by name and you are my mine,' says the Lord.

And, just as he says it to Eve, so he said it to the others – those people we meet in the gospels who, like her, were often afraid because they did not fit in. The young woman called Mary who was to be the mother of the Christ child and the woman called Mary Magdalene who, like Eve, is said to have been a prostitute. 'You are precious in my eyes. You are honoured and I love you.'

He said it to Peter and James and John, to Matthew and to Judas and to the others who made up the twelve. People who smelled of fish and people who wanted to launch an armed rebellion. People who had been swindlers and people who would become betrayers. None of whom, perhaps, would have felt comfortable studying at an English theological college.

So why did Jesus call these people? This strange assortment of the unclean and the improbable? Thinking back to Eve, and why he called her, I suspect there may be two reasons.

One is that they were people of courage. Think back to the event when Jesus calls his first disciples. The call does not come as the result of a church training course or after a deeply spiritual retreat experience. Instead, he is walking along a beach when he sees two men in a fishing boat mending their nets in the sun. Come with me, he says, Come from this place where you are secure and where everything is familiar and follow me to another place where things will look different. Leave your safety zone where you are in control and where you have security and respect. Come with me to the unknown place and meet people who will not care who or what you are.

And, amazingly, they got up and followed him along the beach and into the rest of their lives. They did not know where they were going and what would happen to them. But they went, just as Eve went.

A second reason they were called may be they had an instinctive openness to the love of Jesus. There was an acceptance of God's love which made the risk-taking, and the courage it required, a joy and not an ordeal. Just as Jesus had said in the synagogue: 'The Spirit of the Lord is upon me, for he has anointed me to proclaim good news to the poor', so it seems the Spirit of Christ lives in people like those unwashed and unlikely disciples. And in people like Eve.

The danger is that although Jesus accepted them as they were, we are not willing to do so. Just as we reduce the powerful, passionate and often angry Christ person to a pale figure in a stained glass window, so we dehumanize and disempower the people who were his closest friends. This is particularly true of the women who were among his closest and dearest friends. In a way, both Mary, the mother of Jesus, and Mary Magdalene are effectively banished – one upwards and the other downwards. Mary the mother of Christ is elevated via a romantic medieval view of womanhood. She ceases to be the Palestinian peasant woman of real life and instead becomes the untouchable, unattainable, chastely adored virgin queen of heaven.

Meanwhile Mary Magdalene, the courageous woman who was chosen by God to bring the good news of the resurrection to the disciples, is dismissed as being the woman from whom seven devils were cast out, or (depending on the tradition) a former prostitute.

There is a process of bleaching by which the colour and the humanity is washed out of each of these characters. All we have left is the pale shape of the real person whom Jesus called and loved. Cleanliness is next to godliness, we were taught as children. But that teaching was untrue – Jesus spent his time in the company of the unclean. The most godly people in the gospels smell of fish and sweat and wine. And perhaps some of them smoke and have red nail varnish.

———◆———

WEDNESDAY
THE RAINBOW MAN

One of the blessings of good friends is that you can relax and be yourself in their company. You don't have to try to impress them. Even if you are feeling bad-tempered, there's usually enough love and understanding for it not to matter too much. But sometimes you discover something new about a person you may have known a lifetime.

One of my dearest friends is a parish priest. We will call him Aidan, although that is not his real name, and he is gay. For almost as long as I have known him he has worked in tough inner-city parishes. While I've skipped around doing all sorts of different things, he has continued serving God in the parish. Not in the laborious way a person may struggle with a burdensome duty, but with imagination and dedication – and with laughter. There is armoured glass in the vicarage windows and razor wire round the boundary fence, but his parishioners adore him and his church is full.

One day, while on holiday, he dropped in to see me. As always, we greeted each other with a hug. We talked for a couple of hours over several cups of coffee before it was time for him to leave. As he drove away, I had a strange sense of envy at the way this beloved friend lived his life. I had always admired his ministry; not only the fact he worked so hard, but also because he seemed to be more dedicated than I was. And he seemed to enjoy life immeasurably more than I did. Even so, there was something else which I was only just beginning to realize.

Unconsciously, I suppose, I had always felt a bit sorry for Aidan because he was gay. It was rather like having a good friend who is colour blind – an unfortunate thing to happen to such a good person. However, as he drove away down the vicarage drive, I realized I may have been wrong.

I thought about what it was that made me admire him so much as a priest – and what made me slightly envious of his ministry. Suddenly I realized what it was. He was a more complete person than I am. All these years I had assumed that being gay made him less complete than 'normal' people. What I had just realized was the opposite was true. Aidan is certainly a man, and a braver one than I am in all sorts of ways. But the fact he is gay means there is a significant female element to his nature. He has qualities of character and personality which I do not have, and perhaps cannot have, as a heterosexual man.

I had suddenly realized Aidan was a more complete and balanced human being than me – and most of the other men I know. Instead of being less than whole because of his sexuality, I was suddenly confronted by the possibility that this may actually make him more human and more complete than those of us who are straight. I was reconsidering my years of rather patronizing sympathy for his condition. Perhaps it was me who was colour blind and he who could see rainbows. Live a rainbow life. I had been looking at my beloved friend down a drainpipe for the last 30 years.

--◆--

As I have said, Aidan is not my friend's real name. To reveal that would endanger his employment by the Church. Even though thinking in secular society on gay and lesbian issues has changed over the years, the Church seems stuck uncomfortably in a time warp. It wants to be pastorally caring to all people, and most of the time it tries to avoid being judgemental. But on issues of sexuality, it has a major problem.

Despite the fact that sex is God's method of keeping the human race in existence, and physical expressions of love and companionship seem to be an inescapable part of that process, some people in the Church really would prefer it if sex was abolished. Within the confines of Christian marriage, sex can be tolerated; although there is a residual discomfort about contraception. And about other forms of sexual activity between heterosexual couples which are not designed to result in conception.

The problem is not only that the Church has difficulties with sex in any form, but that gay relations are condemned in some parts of the Bible – notably books of the Old Testament such as Leviticus and in some of the letters of St Paul. People who oppose gay and lesbian relationships are keen to point out these passages. What they are less willing to acknowledge is that other things are equally condemned – the eating of pork and lobster, for example. Meanwhile working on the Sabbath, as we have seen, is such a serious sin, it is punishable by death. Carried to its logical conclusion, we would need to ask for the Archbishop of Canterbury and the Archbishop of York to resign, since it says in the Old Testament that chief priests must be without physical blemish – including their eyesight. And it will be noticed that both archbishops wear glasses.

   This seems to indicate we need to read the scriptures using the brains God gave us, and to ask whether these different passages are still to be taken literally. This does not necessarily mean that stable, loving gay and lesbian relationships are right in the sight of God. It means that they may be, and that people like Aidan may not be as sinful as some Christians believe them to be.

   We need to respect the documents which make up the Bible. But part of that respect is to try to be honest about what we are doing. The words of the Bible arise out of our experience of God. Experience comes first; theology follows and tries to work out the meaning of that experience. Perhaps Aidan is part of our developing experience and part of God's ongoing revelation of himself.

   In his ministry, Aidan hallows God's name and honours his presence in a way which I find awesome. What I have realized is that God may also be hallowing Aidan in all his human wholeness, including his sexuality. He is called by name. Perhaps he is also called by his nature and that nature may be precious to God. People like me need to stop looking at gay and lesbian men and women down the drainpipe of superiority. Who knows, of such may be the Kingdom of Heaven.

———◆———

Day 16   Week 3
THURSDAY
WHAT'S IN A NAME?

There was no doubt about it – Frank Hardwick grew the best roses in the parish. Each year they bloomed strong and red against the blackened walls of the terraced house in the small industrial town where Frank and his wife lived. Red as poppies, said Frank. And he knew all about poppies. Sixty years before, he had been a gunner in the First World War. Now, a dapper elderly man, far into retirement, he seemed quiet and inoffensive. No one would have guessed at the anger that smouldered inside him.

That anger burst out one day when his local priest called to see him. After a few preliminaries about the state of the roses, Frank suddenly said, 'I was in the First World War, you know.'

The priest, unaware of what was coming, made a polite murmur of interest and settled back for what he assumed would be half an hour of gentle reminiscences, images of military bands and old soldiers marching with their medals and umbrellas in the rain at Remembrance Day services. He was jolted wide awake by Frank's first words: 'It was bloody murder out there,' he said. 'Mindless bloody murder.'

Then, for the next hour, with an anger undiminished after 60 years of quiet respectability, he told his story of the fear and carnage of the Great War. How his artillery company had been travelling at night, the gun-carriages drawn by teams of horses. How his company had come under devastating enemy fire. In the darkness and the rain, they could not see what was happening – they could only hear the deafening roar of exploding shells and the screams of horses and men in the blackness and the mud.

At daylight, they found half their company were dead. The next gun-carriage, just a few yards away from Frank's, had vanished – horses, gun and men had been blown into oblivion. With it had been Frank's companions, his mates. Young men, some hardly more than boys, many still in their teens, now pulverized into the bloody mud. Each with a mother waiting at home, many with wives and sweethearts. Every one known by name. Every one loved.

The priest thought back to a book he had once read. It had been written from the enemy viewpoint. A young German infantryman is trapped in a shell-hole during a night attack. Suddenly in the darkness there is the sound of running feet and a body crashes down on top of him. He lunges wildly with his bayonet in the darkness and there is a cry of pain.

As light dawns, he sees he has stabbed a young French soldier. He is slumped in the water and mud at the bottom of the shell crater, covered in blood. Two human beings trapped in a living hell of gunfire and filth. It takes several hours for the French soldier to die. The young German watches in horror as the stranger whom he has stabbed slowly dies before his eyes. He tears open the man's shirt and tries to stop the flow of blood, but it is too late.

As the man dies, his wallet falls out into the mud. There is a photograph and some letters from home. The German soldier picks up the picture of a young woman and a child. In the letters he reads the name of the man he has killed. Then he speaks the simple and terrible words: 'I have killed Gerard Duval, the printer.' Suddenly the whole horror of the Great War is focused on a single moment; a single encounter between two people. They are no longer enemy soldiers fighting for their countries, they are human beings with wives and children. And one of them was a compositor, a printer.

—•—

Whether it is Gerard Duval or Frank Hardwick or Aidan or Eve, the name instantly connects us with the reality of what is happening. It cuts through the deceit of putting uniforms and labels on people and thinking of them in dehumanizing categories: the unemployed, the asylum seekers, the gypsies, the communists. It is easy to fire guns at the enemy or to condemn prostitutes or the homeless. But the moment we have a name, we are recognizing the other person as a living, vulnerable human being.

Perhaps that is one reason why Jesus never went into politics. Standing on the mountain top with the nations of the world spread out before him, he was tempted to use his power for political or military purposes. But that was not his task. Instead of organizing armies and mass movements of faceless men, he was sent to reveal

God's love to human beings who were damaged by systems of power and authority. Living out God's justice, he challenged oppression and evil in the world, and he did this by recognizing and affirming the humanity of the apparently insignificant people he met.

At first sight that may seem to be a pointless exercise: How can love for an individual person affect systems of injustice and oppression? The answer seems to be that systems of injustice and oppression are not impersonal natural disasters which occur like earthquakes. They are an evil created by human beings. They are sustained deliberately for economic and political ends. Love for an individual person is a powerful statement of the truth of the situation – that oppression damages people and they are not social, economic or political objects. When we speak about the gay community or the black community or homeless people, we are talking about human beings of God-given dignity and integrity who are being damaged by other people.

The tragedy and the injustice of Stephen Lawrence's death is more real to us because, in recognizing the name, we engage with the person in an I-and-Thou relationship. In the shell-hole of the society which we have created, in which the vulnerable lives of more than a third of the children in Britain are damaged by needless poverty, we look at each other and see not an alien but another human being, loved by God. And from the recognition of the other person as a vulnerable human being comes the imperative to oppose the injustice which imprisons all of us.

Hallowing the name requires us to hallow the person. It is a responsibility laid on us by the simple act of praying the word 'Abba' to the one who says, 'I have named you by name from your mother's womb. I have written your name on the palms of my hand.'

FRIDAY
THE SPARK OF LIFE

Car batteries are not very big, but they are deceptively heavy. As he drove through the South African township outside Durban, Big John came upon the strange sight of a woman carrying a car battery. He pulled up alongside her and asked where she was taking it. 'To the garage,' she replied.

A mile away, across the valley, was a petrol station. As they drove, Big John discovered why it was so important she got the battery charged. It was the only source of light in the shack dwelling where she and her family lived.

'How much will that cost you?' he asked.

'Three rand,' she replied.

To most people the amount was minimal, but to the people living in the squatter camps, or informal settlement as they are called, it was a large amount of money.

Then Big John had a brainwave. Each day he hitched a flat trailer to his elderly car and visited the camp. Parking on an area of waste ground, he loaded the trailer with car batteries and drove them several miles to his home where he put them on a charger. Then he brought them back. The cost to cover petrol – one and a half rand.

Within weeks dozens of people were having their batteries charged by Big John. Friendships developed and John became a much-loved person in the area. He was accepted by the local leaders, not just because he charged car batteries on the cheap, but because of his kindness, honesty – and gentle humour.

One day Big John happened to ask if there was a church in the area. 'There is not,' they said. They had nowhere to pray.

'Why not build a church?' he said.

'Who will help us?' they replied.

'I am a retired builder,' said John.

'Who will lead the worship?'

'I am a lay assistant at a church in the city,' he said.

Day after day they worked to build the simple structure. Every night the tools and a wheelbarrow provided by John were left unguarded on the site. Even though this precious equipment would have been invaluable to the people living in the area, nothing was ever stolen.

They started holding services long before the church was completed. At first only two or three people came, but gradually the numbers increased. People started to ask to be baptized, so Big John baptized them – signing them with the sign of the cross with his big, rough builder's hands. Eventually there were 79 names in the school exercise book which served as a baptism register.

Each week the church was full, but still the people came.

'We need to extend the church,' they told John. 'Will you help us?'

'No,' said John. 'This is your church now. You must do it for yourselves. You need to take responsibility for your own church.'

And so they did. It had ceased to be Big John's church and become their church.

—◆—

What John had done, almost unconsciously, was to hallow those people he met in the informal settlement. A person of deep faith, he showed them the love and respect of his Lord, not by preaching at them or telling them to get a bus and come to the big church in the city each Sunday, but by helping them to carry their burden. But the strange thing was, in the process of hallowing them, the name of God was being lived out. In Big John's journeying down those dusty roads with his trailer loaded with old car batteries, the presence of God was being quietly proclaimed. The name of God was being honoured.

Of course the people were grateful they did not have to carry the batteries down into the valley and up the other side to the service station. They were glad Big John did not try to make a profit out of them. But most of all they appreciated his willingness to help and the loving friendship he showed in the process.

Without them knowing it, or even John realizing it, the Gospel was being lived out. The good news was being proclaimed to those who, through the violence and greed of others, were condemned to live in poverty. The hallowing and the name went together. In a life dedicated to hallowing the presence of God, Big John was to find his own name and presence hallowed and respected both by those he was able to help, and by others living thousands of miles away.

Listening to Big John's story it is impossible not to hear the echo of the servant ministry of another – not a builder, but a joiner. Kneeling to wash the feet of his disciples at supper, he was hallowing his friends in a simple and memorable act of servanthood.

Loading car batteries onto his trailer and laying roof beams on their church, Big John was hallowing his new-made friends in an equally simple and memorable act of servanthood. In the earthy acts of lifting and building, the love of God was being lived out. Outward and visible signs of God's Kingdom in the dust and dignity of a South African squatter camp.

◄●►

Only a few miles away in the wealthy white-controlled city, people were also going to church. And who is to say God's name was not also being hallowed there? Who knows? All we can do is to ponder the words of the Beatitudes:

Blessed are the poor for theirs is the Kingdom of God.
Blessed are the hungry, for they shall be satisfied.
Blessed are you who weep now, for you shall laugh.
But, alas for you who are rich. You have had your reward already.

I hope that when Big John reads this part of Luke's gospel, he will know he has been hallowing God's name in his own big-hearted way. But I hope he will read further, because there God has something to say to him:

Give and gifts will be given to you. Good measure, pressed down, shaken together, and running over will be poured into your lap. For whatever measure you deal out to others will be dealt to you in return.

Big John has not bought God's favour and reward, but in his instinctive love and care for others he has been hallowing God's name. And by doing that he has opened his own heart to receive the life-giving love of God.

◄●►

Day 18   Week 3
SATURDAY
THE MEMORIAL BARBECUE

Each year, late in the summer, an unusual event took place in the city. It was the memorial barbecue. In a quiet corner of a park a small group of people would meet. They came from different backgrounds – most were living unsettled lives. Some were homeless, others had drink problems. One was a Catholic sister and another, a monk of the Little Brothers of Jesus.

They met every week in a church hall to drink coffee and play darts, dominoes or snooker. To plan holidays together; to share news about friends; to enjoy each other's company. In the summer they would abandon the church hall and meet in the open area of urban parkland which lay alongside one of the main roads into the city. Taking a tape recorder, a camping gas stove and a frying pan they would play music and make bacon and egg sandwiches. For members of the group with secure and stable employment, it was a welcome break from normality.

But towards the end of the summer, they would have a special party in the park. It was the time when they remembered friends who had died in the past year. After the fry-up they would have a quiet time when they called to mind people they had loved. The Catholic sister, who organized the group, had prepared a board with some of the names written on it. Word got round that the event was taking place and, often, people who were not regular members of the group would quietly appear. Something important had drawn them to the small circle of friends.

As they sat, listening to the music, the noise of the passing traffic seemed to recede into the distance. People were invited to add other names of people they knew who had died. Some wrote the names themselves; others, less confident, called out a name and it was written on the board for them. Many of the names were familiar, but others were not. Perhaps they were the names of mothers or fathers, or friends who had died in other cities. People who had died through illness or through violence. People who had been loved and whose names were now being hallowed in a simple and public act of remembrance.

Finally the list was complete and there was a period of quiet. Sometimes there were tears. Someone would pray a prayer. Not the sister or the lay brother, but one of the other group members. It may have been the first time they had spoken a prayer out loud. But perhaps it was not. Many people on the streets live close to God. Finally it was time to go and the cooking utensils, coffee cups and tape recorder were packed up. People drifted away to wherever their lives were taking them; some of them we would not see again. But the board with the names was kept safe.

What had been happening was an alfresco liturgy. Not held on All Souls' Day or in a church building but, nevertheless, a profound act of worship. That anonymous patch of grass under the trees in an urban park was, at least for a moment, a holy place. A place where loving relationships were remembered and names were hallowed.

But that was not all that had been happening. Each person present had been aware the group was honouring and remembering friends who had died. But who were those friends? Not people who were special and different, but ordinary people, like ourselves. And, if they had been loved while they were alive and hallowed now they were dead, then what about those who were still here? Not only was the memorial barbecue a symbolic hallowing of the names and lives of the dead. It was also a powerful affirmation of the worth and significance of the living, especially those people who did not always feel affirmed or hallowed or loved.

—◆—

It is strange how we find it easy to see the good in people when they are dead, but less easy while they are alive. One of the most powerful images of the millennium celebrations was the picture of Nelson Mandela visiting his cell in the prison on Robben Island where he had spent 17 years of his life. He lit a candle and carried it out into the courtyard of the prison, then handed the lighted candle to his successor as president, Thabo Mbeki. A symbol of light and hope in a place which, for years, had been a focus of hatred and oppression.

Mandela, whose name had been ridiculed and held in contempt for years by the political right wing in Britain, was at that moment the most respected and loved person on the planet. That is, in part, because of his great courage in a noble struggle for human freedom, and the quiet dignity and generosity of spirit he showed when he came to power. But maybe it is also because he was old and would soon be dead.

Perhaps it is safer to be generous towards people when they are dead. But the God whose name we hallow is also the God who hallows us, and is generous enough to see the good in us now. The question is, can we see the good in ourselves? Can we, in a good and generous way, hallow the name we have been given? Accept with honest gratitude the people of worth that we are? I think of some people who live fragmented and unsettled lives on the streets, and of others who, despite their obvious gifts and talents, cannot recognize their own worth. They are people who feel no joy at being alive, or any sense of purpose. And yet they are people of wisdom and loving integrity.

But what I do about that, I do not know. All that can be done is to place alongside the emptiness those people seem to feel, the words of the Lord's Prayer. Hallowed be your name. In the quietness of that city park, with the lingering aroma of mown grass and fried bacon, we hallowed the names of those we had loved, and we sensed the hallowing of each other. As we went away, back to our daily lives, in our different ways we felt we had been touched by God. Perhaps for other people whom we love there will also be that sense of hallowing and touch.

THIRD SUNDAY OF LENT
A LABOUR OF LOVE

A row broke out recently over the decision of the Catholic Church in Scotland to offer support for a pregnant 12-year-old schoolgirl. The Church said it was simply responding to a request for help, but pro-abortionists claimed the Church was bribing the child not to have a termination. The pro-abortionists argued the child would not be able to cope with the pregnancy and birth because of her age and immaturity. The Church argued the girl and her family had asked for help and that the foetus was itself an unborn child with a right to life.

Both sides agreed childbirth was a serious issue. But for many couples the seriousness of childbirth only begins to dawn on them long after the pleasure of conception has faded. The advertising industry presents us with images of babies as fragrant and adorable bundles of joy. Seldom are we offered images which reflect reality. From the moment of conception, profound changes take place in the woman's body – and in her relationships with other people. As the pregnancy develops, so the woman's body changes to accommodate the unborn child in the womb. Internal organs are gradually pushed out of their normal position to make room for the foetus and the bones of the pelvic region change their alignment in anticipation of the birth.

Meanwhile the family speaks of the woman 'expecting' and the baby being 'on the way'. For many first-time parents there is little indication of the change that is already taking place in their lives. The baby may well be a bundle of joy, but it will be born with a mind of its own and demands which will have to be met. Inside the womb it has been undergoing the most intensive and important training process it will ever experience – how to survive. It has taken everything it needs from the mother's body. In the latter stages it has wriggled and kicked and punched its way round the womb in preparation for its escape.

At birth it will fill its lungs with air and yell for food. Nothing will ever be the same again. What we have is a very compact, highly

trained person dedicated to staying alive and not remotely interested in what chaos and inconvenience it causes in the process.
Sleepless nights may give the parents an indication of eternity, but
within the blinking of an eye the child will be going to school,
leaving sweaty trainers round the house, going down the pub with
its mates – and suddenly announcing it is 25 years old and leaving
home.

—•—

When Jesus taught his disciples to pray the Lord's Prayer, we do
not know to what extent he talked them through it. Did he simply
give them the words, as Luke recounts, and leave it at that? Or did
he warn them about the implications of using the prayer and
meaning every word? Perhaps he spent a lot of time talking to
them about its meaning. If he did, those conversations have been
lost with the passage of time. But if we, like those disciples, are
serious about our relationship with God, then it is important for
us to think about the meaning – and the dangers – of what we are
saying.

The seemingly harmless words of the third section of the Lord's
Prayer come quietly upon us like a sleeping child, but have all the
force of a tornado when their impact dawns: Your Kingdom come.
Your will be done.

Jesus, sitting with his disciples, has given them the arrow of the
Abba word and then drawn it back deep into the culture and
spirituality of their nation with the words 'hallowed be your
Name'. But now the arrow is released with the first imperative
action words in the prayer: 'Let your Kingdom come. Let your will
be done here among us.'

The familiar words sound harmless enough, but Jesus is
launching a manifesto. God's Kingdom is God's sovereignty, his
rule. The Kingdom is how God wants things to be – and is
determined that things shall be. God's Kingdom is the expression
of the will and purpose of God.

Centuries of tranquil worship in buildings of permanence and
antiquity have encouraged us to assume the Lord's Prayer is also
stable and tranquil. But it is not. To pray that God's will shall be
done is to acknowledge that our own will and desire may have to

be set aside. And that raises the worrying question of who, then, is in control. Of course we know, in theory, that God is more important than we are and that God's will should be done. As long as it is on Sundays and in church. But the possibility that God's will may extend to other days of the week or be operative or relevant outside church buildings is one we hesitate to take seriously.

Praying the Lord's Prayer is like the act of conception. The moment the man releases the sperm into the woman's body, he has lost control of what is happening. The moment the woman's body draws the sperm deep into the warm darkness of the uterus, she too has lost control of what is happening. An independent process is taking place – life. The same thing is happening in the Lord's Prayer. In the act of speaking and meaning those words, we lose control. The moment we truly ask that God's rule and sovereignty will take precedence over our own desires, we are letting go. And we are embarked on that same conception process called life.

But, not only is the idea of trusting God and handing over control a challenging one, it also raises the awkward question of why Jesus should even have included these words in the prayer in the first place. Why do we need to pray that God's will should be put into action and lived out?

The answer seems unavoidable – because the present situation in the world does not reflect the will of God. We are not living God's Kingdom. Things are not the way God wants them to be. There are situations of personal and institutional evil. We say 'Abba', but we do not live out the love of that relationship in the world. To pray 'your Kingdom come' implies that we recognize something needs to arrive which is not here – God's love and passionate concern for justice for all his children. This is the crucial dynamic of the Lord's Prayer – the arrow of God's unconditional love is driven by his deep anger at the injustice of the world.

◄●►

Staring the stark reality of birth and child-rearing in the face, it is little wonder that many women choose to have abortions. That does not make abortion right or wrong, but makes it understandable. Staring the stark reality of the Lord's Prayer in the face and recognizing the implications of what we are saying, it is little

wonder that many Christians abort the Abba process. We instinctively put ourselves first. We withdraw into a process of denial
whereby we simply do not engage with the meaning of what Jesus
was telling his disciples. But, if we cannot bear to confront the
reality of the Jesus prayer, how can we seriously ask to be his
disciples?

Day 20   Week 4
MONDAY
THE LAW-BREAKER

From Monday to Friday the old Victorian church building
remains locked. Not only is the heavy wooden door bolted, but
there is also a wrought-iron security gate on the porch, fastened
with a large padlock.

The building looks more like a fortress than a place of
encounter with the living God and the stonework, blackened by
a hundred years of factory smoke and pollution, gives little indication of the joy of the Resurrection. But most people walking
past are well aware of the reason for the bolted door and the
security gate. This is an area with a very high incidence of crime.
Unemployed and anti-social young men are suspected of being
the chief perpetrators.

Entering the church each Sunday, most of the worshippers
leave the social problems of the area behind them as they kneel in
prayer. In front of them, in the stained glass of the east window,
the Crucifixion is depicted. It seems to have little connection with
the lives of many of the people in the streets outside. It may be
that few, if any, of the Sunday worshippers have thought about the
reason why the person on the cross in front of them was executed.
But for the people who put him to death, he was an unemployed,
anti-social young man. And he was certainly a law-breaker. Why
else would he have deserved death?

---◆◆---

The suggestion that Jesus may have been a law-breaker triggers a remarkable reaction in many Christians. Their assumption is that, since he spent most of his time either healing people or telling them about God, he somehow must have been respectful of authority – a model citizen. But you only have to read the gospels to realize this was not always so.

There are many occasions when he is seen breaking the strict code of religious law, and at other times he challenges deeply respected traditions in such a way as to earn the hatred of the political and religious leaders. The fact that he did not commit crimes such as theft or murder, does not mean his law-breaking was unimportant. His actions were profoundly threatening to the stable order of society.

Repeatedly we see him breaking the law of the Sabbath. Time after time he is shown healing people on that sacred day, despite the fact that this disregard for the law was a very serious matter. In some parts of the Old Testament, such a crime is punishable by death. On numerous other occasions, he is portrayed eating with prostitutes and sinners and he and his disciples are criticized for disregarding the important food hygiene laws.

In his comments on marriage and divorce, we see him challenging the powerful gender assumption that men are superior in rank and importance to women. What is often taken to be simply a condemnation of divorce is also a reversal of the oppressive custom by which a man could arbitrarily divorce his wife by a note of dismissal, thereby ruining her life. Instead Jesus endorses equality of the genders by saying that if either brings a divorce, then both are guilty.

In other instances he appears to challenge the assumption that foreigners are excluded from the blessings of God's love and from involvement in his work. Time and time again we see Jesus singling out people from other communities and revealing them as used by God in his work in the world. Not only does he cause offence by doing this, he also presents the chosen people of his own nation as having failed in their calling and being by-passed by God. Thus the despised foreigner, a Samaritan, is the one who shows love, after the priest and the Levite conspicuously fail to help the wounded man.

The rabble from the streets are asked to the wedding banquet when the formerly invited guests fail to come to the celebration; the salt which has lost its flavour is thrown out; and the tree which fails to bear fruit is cut down. The rich, whose wealth was regarded as a sign of blessing, are told their money is a barrier between them and God. The religious leaders are told prostitutes will enter God's Kingdom – while they will be excluded.

We pray the words 'Your will be done', but how can we know God's will? We may want to bring about the Kingdom, but what are its marks? What does such a process involve? Perhaps the answer lies in the person of Christ himself. In the Lord's Prayer, the arrow of God's love is driven, as we have seen, by the loving concern that all his children should enjoy justice and fulfilment. This powerful dynamic mirrors exactly Jesus' own sense of being sent: 'Armed with the power of the Holy Spirit,' Jesus identifies his own purpose and commission with the words: 'He has sent me to proclaim good news to the poor . . .'

Christ is, himself, the living out of God's Kingdom. God's rule in its human expression and directed to the concerns that express God's will. However, with the passing of the centuries, there are inevitable changes in social context – we do not feel strongly about working on Saturdays; and eating lobster and pork is not a big issue for most of us. We need to hear what Jesus is saying and apply that to our own world, and to do that we need to look at the overall picture of his words and actions.

As we do this, a clear picture emerges of someone at ease with the marginalized and the outcast; and in constant conflict with the powerful and orthodox religious. He appears as a person who takes delight in eating with sinners; who allows a prostitute to wash and to kiss his feet; who embraces the defiled and defiling leper in a spontaneous expression of compassion and solidarity; who refuses to judge others; who reverses the accepted order of society so that children, women and the weak come before the male and the powerful.

In challenging the accepted and deep-seated traditions of his day and, on many occasions, deliberately breaking the law, we realize this person does not simply tell his followers how to pray – he shows them how to live this unsettling prayer. He does not simply launch the Abba concept like an arrow from a bow – he himself is the arrow of God. But it is an arrow which carries a lifeline of hope and not the sentence of death. Like a lifeline fired from the shore to a stricken ship, it carries the vital thread of life.

The Christ person is the human expression of God's Kingdom. He is the only one with the authority to speak the Abba word – and the only one who can give us permission to use that powerful word ourselves. Jesus the law-breaker is also Jesus the life-giving Christ. He is both messenger and message. But on which side of a locked church door will we encounter him?

Day 21   Week 4
TUESDAY
THE PAIN-SHARER

It was raining heavily and the homeless man's clothes were soaked through when he arrived at the day centre. The shoes he was wearing had split open and it was clear he needed a complete change of clothing. A priest, working as a part-time volunteer in the clothing store at the day centre, helped him off with his coat and found a chair for him. The man struggled to untie his shoe laces and the priest stooped to help.

As he removed the first sodden and broken shoe, the most appalling smell filled the room. The man had probably not taken his shoes off in months. The foot of the woollen sock had disintegrated and the flesh of several of the man's exposed toes appeared to have rotted away. A combination of constant soaking through sleeping rough and poor circulation due to chronic ill health had created a condition like trench foot, suffered by troops in the flooded trenches of the First World War.

With some reluctance the homeless man was persuaded to see the day-centre medical team. Meanwhile the priest searched for a pair of shoes from among the clothing store's meagre stock of second-hand footwear. There was nothing that would fit. In a city that boasted it was the most dynamic and successful urban centre outside London, a man with rotting feet had no shoes to wear. Angry and frustrated, the priest set off into the city centre to buy a broad-fitting pair of shoes for the homeless man.

As he walked he thought of the obscene sight of the man's foot: how the fibres of the woollen socks seemed to have rotted into the man's flesh; the embarrassed silence as the shoes were removed and the unforgettable smell that had filled the room; how very careful he had been to wash his hands after that finger-tip contact with the man's feet. Maybe he should have washed the man's feet. As a priest, wasn't that his job? That's what they would be doing at the medical centre, though perhaps wearing rubber gloves.

As he walked through the November rain, he thought of another man with rotting flesh who was despised, through no fault of his own, by the people of another city. How he had come to Jesus and asked to be healed – to be given life. He was called a leper and, whether or not the disease was technically leprosy, the effect was the same. He was made to ring a bell and shout 'unclean' as he approached. Contact with such a person was forbidden. To associate with such a person would make you defiled and therefore, it was said, unable to worship God. The leper was a total outcast – socially and spiritually.

The priest thought about the different gospel accounts of the healing of the leper and how each account included a seemingly unnecessary detail. When Jesus saw the leper, he was filled with a deep and compassionate anger at the man's suffering. He did not respond with the professional detachment of a medical team – he did not wear rubber gloves. He had not needed to go near the leper in order to heal him. He could have simply spoken the word – but he did not. Instead, Jesus reached out and touched him.

In that moment of instinctive, loving compassion, the Son of God was defiled by the defiling flesh of the leper. The rule by which no religious person should ever be defiled was broken by the one who was the human expression of God's will – of the Kingdom.

St Mark says Jesus reacted in 'warm indignation' to the man's suffering. That means he was not a detached observer considering an interesting medical case. He was a human being touched by the pain of another person's suffering. He felt the pain of the injustice and the oppression the man had been made to suffer – as well as the pain of the disease itself. Reading the story we oversimplify what was going on. We assume Jesus was concerned only with the healing of the individual. But he was also concerned with the system of bogus purity which kept the man trapped in a dehumanizing ghetto of separate existence. By speaking the words of healing, the man was made whole. By touching the man, a system of injustice was being exposed and challenged.

As he walked, the priest realized how the situation at the day centre had brought alive the significance of this gospel story which he had read a thousand times. Now, tramping through the city streets, he was experiencing a fragment of its power and its meaning. The pain of the leper; the pain of the injustice; the pain of the Christ person. The smell of the gospel; and the cost of the love.

But why the cost of the love? Because to touch the leper was to break the rules. And breaking the rules carried with it a penalty. Suddenly other parts of the gospel accounts started to have a new significance. Repeatedly in the gospels we hear the ominous warning that the religious leaders had 'taken offence' at Jesus and were plotting to have him killed. They were plotting his execution, not because he was a healer, but because he opposed the injustice of the religious system and challenged their power over people's lives. 'You lay a religious burden on people which they cannot bear,' Jesus once told the chief priests. Instead of helping people to come to know God, you put barriers in their way.

As he walked, the priest began to realize that the pain he was feeling at the suffering and degradation of his homeless friend was a glimpse of the pain Jesus felt in a hundred different situations of suffering and injustice in the gospels. For the first time he began to realize that, when Jesus said things like, 'I was naked and you did not clothe me, hungry and you did not share your food', he might have been feeling the pain of that rejection. When he stood on the hillside overlooking the city and wept for its people, he was feeling the pain of his rejection – and of their future suffering.

——•——

There is a danger that we reduce the idea of God's Kingdom to a religious theory. Like the priest at the day centre, we need to be open to the possibility that we encounter Christ in our neighbour and we discover the meaning of life in the pain of those brave people we call poor.

Returning to the clothing store, the priest knew that, for once, he was living the gospel from the inside. In a fragmentary way he had felt the pain of both the leper and the Christ person. And gradually he was coming to realize whose feet would wear the shoes.

——•——

Day 22   Week 4

WEDNESDAY

THE FROG AND THE HAIRDRYER

Eve rang again today. Things are going better and she may yet survive. The college is the poshest place she and the children have ever seen. Set in the leafy suburbs with its own extensive lawns, it is nothing like the terraced street of the inner city where they lived before. While we are talking there is a sudden commotion. The children have come in, carrying a frog they had found in the garden. They are also carrying the hairdryer. I listen spellbound to the conversation going on in the college flat.

'Oh look,' says Eve, 'they've found a frog. I've never seen a frog before. The only things they used to bring in at home were the used syringes people used to chuck over the wall.'

There is a pause. Then, 'What are you doing with the hairdryer?' There is the muffled sound of a child's voice. Then Eve yells, 'No, don't dry it with the hairdryer. Frogs are supposed to be wet.' Exit two small children and a much relieved frog.

Is this young woman with her red nail varnish and children who try to blow-dry a damp frog really going to be ordained a priest in the Church of England? A few weeks ago she wrote to her friend the Archbishop of Canterbury, sending him some pictures of the children and telling him how she was getting on. A week later she got a letter back from one of the assistant bishops at Lambeth, and was much impressed. Then a couple of days ago she got a personal letter from the Archbishop himself. It is not often you hear about people crying with happiness. I am not sure what the college thinks of all this.

Meanwhile, we have to ask what we think of it. Is Eve's story just an odd little episode which has happened by chance? The probability is she will not finish the course and will drop back into the urban obscurity from which she came. On the other hand, just how probable is God?

With each day that passes, this young woman is getting stronger in her faith and more deeply rooted in the love of God. I listen to her voice on the phone, delighting in her enthusiasm and her uncertainties – but also listening for the deeper resonances of what is happening in the college community around her. Will she be rejected by students who do not understand her and may despise her background? For the first few days, other students kept asking what sort of course her husband was doing. But there is no husband – and they could not grasp the possibility that she herself had been recommended for training for ordination.

But now things seem to be changing. There has been a problem with the children's schooling. The local school was far too middle class for them, so Eve enrolled them at an inner-city church school several miles away. They have settled in well, but there is a transport problem. How do they get to school, when Eve does not drive and has no car? For the past few weeks they have been going by taxi – and Eve has been running out of cash. But now the other students have organized a rota of people with cars to take the children to school. Gentle ripples of care and support. Quiet signals of hope.

But what else is happening? Where is God in this and what has it to do with the Kingdom? For some years, Eve came to see me for what is called spiritual direction. That means you help the other person to sort out their relationship with God – usually by listening as carefully as possible to what they are saying, and interfering in their friendship with God as little as you can. It is more like a companionship in faith than one person telling the other how to be holy.

My spiritual direction of Eve lasted for about 20 minutes. Then, with a smile, God turned the tables. Since then, I have learnt more about God from this formerly abused and prostituted young woman than anyone else I have ever met. Occasionally taking a break for her to have a fag, we would engage in long conversations about God and about the city. About how the Church could be more prophetic, or challenging in a Jesus-ish sort of way.

Each time we met I felt I was being touched by the Kingdom of God. And each time we talk on the phone the same thing happens. Somewhere in her damaged and nightmarish past something very strange has happened to Eve. Instead of becoming more defensive and hiding herself away behind a protective mask, she has become even more open and honest. One moment she is like a little child and the next, like a wise old woman.

It makes me think back to the way Jesus spoke about the people who were his followers, 'these little ones', he said. Women and men who were not highly educated and who did not have the airs and graces of the social elite – but perhaps had the same direct and open honesty that Eve has.

No wonder Jesus took a small child and stood it in front of the crowd and told them, 'Only if you become like this child, will you enter the Kingdom.' What he seemed to be saying was that it was only if we have the open and honest trust of a child, will we truly be able to say 'Abba' and to receive the life-giving love of God. But perhaps he was also saying something else – that children have a natural and innate spiritual awareness which education by school and family often destroys. Perhaps Jesus was not saying that God only wants kids in the Kingdom of Heaven – but that the only people with the openness and honesty to receive the love of God are those with the child-like trust of the young. The problem with trust is that it makes you vulnerable, but without vulnerability there is no love. And without love we are all dead.

Day by day, Eve knows that she is vulnerable. Perhaps that is one reason why she is a sign of God's Kingdom.

Day 23   Week 4

THURSDAY

THE RISK-TAKER

The man was becoming increasingly worried about getting to work 40 miles away in Manchester. It was snowing and already the drive was blocked by a deep drift. It was certain he would not be able to use the motorway. He phoned the station to see if any trains were running. At the moment they are still getting through, said the voice on the other end of the line. Taking no risks, he got out his thickest pullover, his heavy overcoat and his boots and set off to walk the mile and a half to the station. He arrived half an hour later, covered in snow and within minutes was on the train. He felt pleased with himself.

As he got off the train in Manchester, however, he was aware people were looking at him strangely. As he walked out of the station he realized that, while it may have been snowing heavily at home, it was not snowing in Manchester. In fact it was a dry and sunny day. Feeling like something from another planet, he walked down the main street and into the office, to be met by a round of applause from his amused colleagues.

People taking part in some rather unusual city-centre prayer events called Retreats on the Streets often go through a similar risk-limitation process. These urban retreats are a way of using the city as a resource for prayer and a place of encounter with God. The idea is that people spend a day in the city with nothing to do, other than be aware of what is happening around them and to reflect on the fact that the people in the city, rich and poor, are all God's children. During the day, which they spend alone, they become aware of the vast differences in power and wealth which exist side by side in the city. It is an exercise in social justice awareness.

Above all, they are asked to leave all their belongings behind them at the city-centre church which is used as a retreat centre. Cash, credit cards, cheque books, diaries, keys and reading materials are all removed from them. All they are allowed to take with them is 50 pence – the price of a cheap cup of coffee. That has to last them from 9.30 in the morning until 6.30 at night when they are allowed back into the church. In taking part in the retreat, they are not pretending to be poor but, by handing over their possessions, they are in a symbolic way placing themselves alongside people who, day by day, have no money and very few choices. They are trying to take seriously the commandment to love God and their neighbour. For a few hours at least, they are attempting to walk in their neighbour's shoes.

Sometimes, to minimize the imaginary risks of the day, they come overdressed with thick jumpers, boots and thermal underwear. And sometimes, like the man on the train, they find the weather takes an embarrassing turn for the better. But no matter how ill-judged their wardrobe, they are doing something important – they are walking in the footsteps of Christ. In handing over their money and possessions at the start of the event, their actions mirror those of the Christ person who laid aside his power to be born into the world. As the writer of the Letter to the Philippians says,

> though the divine nature was his from the first; yet he did not think to snatch at equality with God, but made himself nothing, assuming the nature of a slave. Bearing the human likeness,

revealed in human shape, he humbled himself and accepted death – death on a cross.

The interesting thing is that what we wear and where we walk changes our view of the world. No doubt things look different from the back seat of a chauffeur-driven Rolls Royce or from the balcony of Buckingham Palace. They look different, not only because of the physical position they place you in, but also because of the power position. Walking the city streets on their urban retreat, people are often accosted by someone begging. But for once in their lives, there is no question as to what they should do. They do not have money to give or withhold. And that can be remarkably liberating. Instead of walking past with a pang of guilt or irritation, they can honestly say, 'I'm sorry, I don't have any money on me.' And some amazing conversations have ensued from that simple statement.

People taking part in the retreat then discover for themselves that homeless people on the streets are often intelligent, articulate, kind and deeply aware of the presence of God. One woman returned from her day on the streets and said, 'My eyes have been opened. I have lived in this city all my life and I never knew what was there in front of my eyes. Things will never be the same for me again.'

But what was it that had opened not only her eyes, but those of hundreds of others who have had the courage to risk a retreat on the streets? A very limited experience of vulnerability and a gentle but serious attempt to walk for a day with the Lord. How strange that the person many of us believe to be the human expression of God chose to be vulnerable for almost the whole of his life.

Born at risk in a stable; fleeing as a refugee into Egypt; leaving the security of his home in Nazareth to walk into the wilderness and the unknown; adopting the life of an itinerant preacher and teacher, often with nowhere safe to sleep; befriending people who were themselves vulnerable and at risk, he was consequently in conflict with the religious and political authorities; finally being arrested, and condemned to death.

So why, if he himself is God's Kingdom working itself out in the world, did he choose to be vulnerable? What does that say about the nature of God? It gives a new meaning to the saying that God is love. Instead of that love being handed down on a silver plate from heaven, we suddenly glimpse the love of God being lived out below us in the gutter. The friends Jesus chose were almost always the humble and the poor. The people he shared food and drink with were often those rejected by the religious and the self-opinionated as the scum of the earth.

But, if he befriended them then, perhaps he is also befriending them now. Spending a day on the streets meeting his sort of people may not be such a crazy idea after all. Little wonder that people come back from their day with the feeling they have come very close to God.

—◆—

Day 24   Week 4

<h1 style="text-align:center">FRIDAY</h1>

<h2 style="text-align:center">DISHONEST TO GOD?</h2>

Some time ago a leading Christian children's charity enraged many members of the Church of England by its decision to consider allowing gay and lesbian people to foster or adopt some of the children it worked with. The argument was that these young people needed the best available placement in order to recover from the damage they had suffered in their lives. From its wide experience of child care, The Children's Society argued there were times when such a placement might be with a person or a couple who were gay or lesbian.

The reaction was immediate. Many people applauded what they saw as a courageous and just decision, but others saw the decision as a betrayal of Christian values and a denial of scripture. One elderly person wrote in with a very telling comment: 'You have gone against something which we have been brought up all our lives to believe.'

Whether the charity's decision was a denial of scripture or

whether it was a prayerful living out of the love of God is a question that, for the moment, we need to leave on one side. The issue for us now is whether we have the right to question long-held beliefs and assumptions about God. Are we, as intelligent and honest people, permitted to ask any question – or are some issues and doctrines so basic and time-honoured that they are sacrosanct?

—•—

When we say the words of the Lord's Prayer and ask that God's Kingdom will come, there is an implicit hope that God's sovereign rule will come about in this world as well as in heaven. But if we are to look for signs of God's Kingdom here on earth, where might we discern this process taking place? If Christ is the human expression of the will and purpose of God – an expression of God's Kingdom – then what evidence is there of his presence in the world? Do we see God's Kingdom in the Church? Here we come up against an awkward question: How honest is the Church? The Church does not claim to be God's Kingdom on earth, but it does call itself the Body of Christ.

When Jesus broke the bread at the Last Supper and said, 'This is my body', he was saying the bread was a symbol, or an expression, of his whole self. That the breaking and sharing of this bread were a sign of his sharing and giving of himself. All that he was.

Twenty or thirty years later, in his letters to the young churches, however, St Paul develops the idea of the 'body' of Christ by using the term to describe the Church. 'We are the Body of Christ,' he said. 'We were all baptized into one body.'

Admittedly Paul was working out his theology in response to real-life situations – the Christians at Corinth were behaving appallingly and part of Paul's task was to restore some sense of order to those particular people. He was not writing an all-embracing theology to last for the next 2,000 years. But his letters have lasted, and there is a danger that we read them out of their historical and social context.

Even in Paul's own day there must have been serious questions about what he was saying. When we look at Jesus in the Gospel accounts, we see someone whose relationships are typically open and inclusive. Apart from his criticisms of the religious and political authorities, he is remarkably non-judgemental. The meals he shared with others were expressions of acceptance and fellowship rather than social politeness. They were open to the most controversial characters. Hence the repeated criticisms that he ate with tax collectors and sinners. The central act of worship of the Church, the Eucharist or Communion, derives directly from these meals and from the Last Supper. The Eucharist, however, is an exclusive act which almost always draws a line between the initiated members of the Church and outsiders.

In calling itself 'the body' of Christ, the Church is in fact using a prime model of exclusiveness. A body is a finite organism enclosed in an envelope of skin. Objects and materials pass in and out of the body in limited and highly controlled ways – nourishment, sexual activity and waste disposal. By defining itself as the Body of Christ, the Church is actively or tacitly making claims to a privileged and exclusive position of power and authority. It is in danger of claiming it is the one valid and authentic route of access to God. The old slogan 'no salvation outside the Church' is little used now, but the inference is still there. Drainpipe theology is alive and well.

But what happens when we look at the reality of the Church here on earth? The birth of Christ indicates that God is involved and active in the world in a process called the Incarnation. So what about the Church? How 'incarnational' of the Kingdom is the Church?

The way the Church has lived out its faith over the last 2,000 years raises doubts as to how far it has lived out God's rule – the Kingdom of God. The history of the Church in South Africa is an example of the way the Church has denied the Kingdom, and colluded with evil in colonial exploitation and the apartheid system, which was its economic outcome. While a minority of white Christians opposed the apartheid regime from the start, many churches either supported the oppression of the black population or adopted a position of false neutrality.

In recent years, calls for reconciliation between the two sides in the struggle sounded like an appeal to the Christian ideal of peace. But, by not having the integrity to name the evil of apartheid, these church people were in fact siding with the powerful white regime and perpetuating the injustice of the status quo. It was only in 1986 that many of these churches came off the fence with the publication of what was called the *Kairos* (moment of truth) document. This acknowledged corporately that the apartheid system was a structural evil which stood against the Kingdom of God and that neutrality was not a Kingdom option.

By supporting apartheid, or colluding with it, many churches were denying the love of God and the Christ person who is the visible expression of that love. What meaning does it then have, in the real world, to say that such churches were the Body of Christ? Meanwhile, when we see the way in which some secular groups participated in the struggle against apartheid, we may ask whether they were not living out the inclusive love of Christ? Perhaps this gives new meaning to the words of Jesus: 'Only those who do the will of my heavenly Father will enter the Kingdom' and 'My mother and my brothers are those who hear the word of God and act upon it.'

Perhaps we need to rethink our understanding of the Church as the Body of Christ, and to consider the possibility that many people outside the formal Church may be working for the justice and righteousness of God and, thereby, living out the spirit of Christ. Some may be atheists who reject the very concept of God. Others may be people who are gay or lesbian. They, too, may be doing the will of our heavenly Father. But that is not what we have always been brought up to believe.

Day 25   Week 4
SATURDAY
IT'S TOUGH BEING A DAD

Parents have it tough these days – especially fathers. What seems to have happened naturally and without comment for several million years has suddenly become a matter of great debate. And anxiety. Parenthood is not as easy as first appears. Bonding between fathers and sons is reckoned to be an area of particular difficulty. And so it was that we decided to build the wall.

Partly because of the layout of the vicarage garden, and partly because of the amount of time I spent dealing with church affairs instead of giving 'quality time' to my children, we decided on a project to build a stone wall. The lawn, such as it was, sloped away from the house in an easterly direction. The problem was that, on the rare occasions we sat out, we found ourselves either not facing the sun, or sitting sideways to the slope of the lawn. The answer was to build a low wall across the lawn at right angles to the slope. Then fill in behind the wall and grass the flat surface we had created. We would then have a flat lawn where we could face the sun without falling sideways off our chairs. The planning and construction of this simple wall would be carried out by me and my young son, Ben. It would be a good way of spending time together – male bonding.

First, we marked out the line of the wall, then dug a trench for the foundations. We collected a large amount of stone and started building. After some time my elder daughter, who happens to be an architect, drifted over and looked down into the trench. She had a pensive look in her eye. 'Dad,' she eventually said. 'Do you know, there are cathedrals in this country that have foundations shallower than that?'

But she is a girl and we are boys and we were busy with our building. We did not listen. After several weeks we had used up much of our stock of stone, and the wall had almost reached ground level. As the months went by what had started as a great adventure began to feel more like an ordeal. Ben found he had probably had enough of bonding and went off to play on his bike.

Meanwhile, I began to realize we had used the best stones first. The ones that remained were misshapen and needed cutting. Cutting stone sounds easy, but it is not. It involves hammering the stone with an implement called a cold chisel. If you are lucky the stone splits and produces the squared shape you need. If you are not lucky, or skilful, the hammer hits the back of your hand. Either that or you realize the stone is so hard that nothing is going to make any impression on it. But stone is not easy to come by and it is very heavy to carry, and so you keep trying.

Eventually, the Great Wall Crisis was resolved when I was rushed into hospital in the middle of the night with a ruptured appendix. Suddenly it was OK not to be building walls. Instead I paid my elder son Nick to come and do the job for me. Ben suddenly showed renewed interest in the project – and the money. Whichever it was, the pair of them completed the wall with annoying ease.

--•--

Watching from the lounge window as I waited for my stitches to heal, I suddenly began to understand the meaning of the phrase in the gospels about 'the stone the builders rejected', and why it was important.

Why should a builder reject a stone? Two thousand years ago suitable rock must have been just as hard to come by, and just as heavy to carry. Why would you throw away a stone if you were building a wall? What was the reason I had thrown stones away, out on the vicarage lawn? Because they did not fit – and were too difficult to cut to shape. There is no other reason why you would reject a stone.

But if Jesus referred to himself as the stone which the builders rejected, what did that mean? Simply he was the wrong shape – and they could not change him. He did not fit in their wall.

Out on the vicarage lawn, if a stone did not fit, then it meant the stone was the problem. Whatever else my daughter might think about foundations, there was nothing wrong with my wall. But Jesus is the human face of God. He is the Kingdom lived out. In John's gospel we hear the tremendous words: 'In the beginning was the Word and the Word was with God and the Word was God.' And the Word he is speaking about was the Word at that moment being born into the world – Jesus. A little later, the writer shows us Jesus as saying, 'whoever sees me, sees the one who sent me'.

If we take those words seriously, then we are led to the conclusion that if he does not fit, then there is something wrong with the wall of religious law the ruling priestly group had constructed over the years. And he did not fit. St John says so. 'He entered his own realm, but his own would not receive him,' says John. Instead they crucified him.

He did not fit with the powerful political and religious leaders then, but how well does he fit with the powerful now? How easily does the stone rejected by the builders for being too sharp and misshapen fit with our powerful, wealthy and largely middle-class religious establishment?

How shall we measure and model our own lives? By a conformity to the powerful religious system which the Church has become – or by holding before us the hard and irregular stone which the builders rejected? Religious systems always seem to want things to be smooth – the culture, the liturgy, and the pronouncements of the Church are typically smooth and rounded. But Jesus is a rough diamond who does not always fit with our religious systems.

Choose him and we shall find life. But like him we shall also be bruised and rejected by the builders. It is a hard choice God offers us.

FOURTH SUNDAY OF LENT
THE GIFT OF GOD

The people who write travel brochures have an unenviable task. How many different ways can you describe blazing sun and golden beaches? Unless you are inspired, as was the person writing the description of a holiday apartment on a little-known Greek island. After the inevitable comments about azure blue sea and friendly locals came the wonderful words: Five minutes' walk from the village bakery. We booked that very day. It is one thing to be able to imagine the sea and to look forward to lazing on the beach, but this time you could smell new-baked bread.

Why is it that bread, which we take for granted at home as being little more than the boring stuff holding the cucumber and tuna together, can somehow become a feast when eaten in the morning sun on the balcony of a holiday villa? Perhaps because, when we make the time, we discover the importance of the simple things in life.

How strange that something as ordinary as bread should be given such an important place in the Lord's Prayer. The first three sections of the prayer focus on God. First comes the all-important Abba petition which inspires the entire prayer. Then comes the humble petition that the presence and reality of God should be reverenced and hallowed. Out of this profound acknowledgement of God's overarching presence, Jesus launches us forward into the Kingdom dynamic: May God's sovereignty and rule be increasingly realized here and now in our lives.

But now the prayer changes – the focus moves from God to ourselves with a series of petitions asking that we may receive life. And the first petition is about bread. It is a simple request: Give us food. But, as with the simple sounding word, 'Abba', we are in deep water. The words of the prayer, as we have received it, actually say: 'Our bread for tomorrow, give us today.' But what we are dealing with here is not a simple shopping list request, but a kaleidoscope of meanings.

Whether or not the disciples accepted the prayer in holy silence or whether they interrogated Jesus about the meaning of the words he had given them, we do not know. Human nature being what it is, however, we may assume that for the next few months, probably over numerous glasses of wine, they talked about the meaning of this deceptively simple sentence. It is to be hoped they did, because they were to hear echoes of this prayer in the pain and despair which lay ahead for all of them. But all that is in the future, for us as well as for them. For now, let us try to explore just a few of the threads of meaning in the words which many of us have spoken every day of our lives.

First of all, the prayer speaks of bread; our most basic food. When Jesus was starving in the wilderness, the first temptation was the offer of bread. Centuries ago, lost in the desert, the migrant tribe of the Hebrews received manna from heaven; the gift of food from God to keep them alive on their great trek. Bread by which we will survive. At its most basic level, the prayer is asking that we might be given the means of survival. Let us live.

Second, with the word 'give' the prayer acknowledges that life is a gift of God. Lord, let us receive your gift of life. We are alive by the gift, or grace as it is sometimes called, of God. Place your hand on your chest and feel your heart beating. Each moment your heart beats, you are being held in life by the grace of God. No wonder the primary act of worship of the Church is called the Eucharist – thanksgiving.

Third, the prayer speaks of 'us' and not me. It is a corporate or communal prayer. We speak the words in the fellowship of others. This is not a drainpipe prayer, it is a sunrise prayer – let your life-giving love fill us all with life. We recognize not only our own need but the need of others. Not only our own humanity, but the humanity of our neighbour. Again we feel the pulse of the word 'Abba' and sense the love which enfolds us all.

But now things get more complicated – our bread for tomorrow. What does that mean? If the prayer was spoken in the evening, it may simply mean the food we will need when we get up to do our work in the morning. But 'tomorrow' also has the overtone of

something else: the Great Tomorrow – the end of time when God
will bring the present age to an end. In this context, bread for
tomorrow means the bread of life – a phrase used by Jesus to
describe himself. A phrase indicating the hope and possibility of
eternal life.

The request ends, however, with the word 'today' placed oddly
at the end of the sentence to give it more emphasis. This is really
important because what it does is to link the deep and mysterious
echoes of the idea of the bread of life and the Great Tomorrow
with present reality. The prayer seems to be saying let the promise
of eternal life happen here and now – today. With that single
word, the false distinction between the spiritual and the material
is removed. We are not asking for pie in the sky when we die. We
are being told to ask that God's promise of eternal life, life in all
its fullness, will break in on us today.

And that has a very familiar ring to it. Remember the meals
which Jesus shared with the unclean and the outcast? The meals
which brought him into such bitter conflict with the religious
authorities? Why were the clergy so angry with what Jesus was
doing? Because they knew, as he knew, that there was deeper
meaning to that shared bread than simply people filling their
stomachs.

Jesus was sharing physical food, but by doing so he was offering
them the bread of life – the bread for the Great Tomorrow. How?
Simply by saying that in sharing food, he was sharing friendship
– and his friendship was God's friendship. These ordinary, earthly
meals were hallowed. They were Abba meals – meals which carried
a powerful coded message. The message was that, despite their
defilement and inability to conform to the religious law, the people
with whom Jesus was sharing food were loved unconditionally by
God. They were receiving the gift of life. Remember what Jesus
said to Zacchaeus when he went to the swindling tax collector's
home for supper and shared bread with him? 'Salvation has come
to this house today.' Salvation means life – today and in the Great
Tomorrow.

◄●►

Sitting on the balcony of our holiday apartment eating bread still warm from the bakers and drinking freshly ground coffee, we are experiencing a hint of what Jesus meant.

———•———

Day 27   Week 5
MONDAY
BREAD FOR THE WORLD

It is fascinating how words change their meanings with the passage of time. For example, there is a word in the Church of England's 1662 Book of Common Prayer which we read as 'prevent'. The impression is that we are asking God to prevent or stop us doing something. However, the meaning of the word when it was first written was completely different. Then the word meant 'to go before'.

Since not everyone uses the Book of Common Prayer these days, this may not be a life-and-death situation. However, there is misunderstanding of a much more important word and this *is* a matter of life and death. The word is 'peace'.

To us in everyday usage, the word peace carries the idea of tranquillity and quietness – the absence of conflict. It is a word much loved by the Church, but only in that popular rendering. The problem is, the word 'peace' does not mean tranquillity when we speak of the peace of God or the peace which the Christ person intends. In fact, as with the word prevent, almost the opposite is true. The word peace on the lips of Jesus means vibrant well-being and fullness of life – the overflowing blessings of life which God intends for all of us. But we live in a world where most people are denied well-being or fullness of life. So to pray for God's peace means asking for anything but quietness and tranquillity. It means asking for – and committing ourselves to – change and action.

When we pray the words of Christ in the Lord's Prayer, 'Give all of us today our daily bread' or 'The bread for tomorrow, give us today', our prayer has dramatic political and economic implications. Archbishop Helder Camara once said, 'When I give bread to the hungry, they call me a saint. But when I ask why the hungry have no bread, they call me a communist.'

The words of the Lord's Prayer are Abba words; words which acknowledge the all-embracing love of God for every one of us. Held within this life-giving and life-creating love, we are asking that we all might receive the blessing of life and, by implication, remove the barriers to that life. Helder Camara knew only too well that giving a loaf of bread to the poor might feed a person physically for a day. But it was also a subtle way of keeping that person quiet – and trapped in the silent prison of poverty.

What Camara condemned, and what the Church often applauds, was the patronizing act of doling out a ration of food to the poor while still retaining power and control over that person's life. Holding that person in political or economic captivity.

Camara knew that was a denial of human dignity and human rights, as well as being a denial of the Gospel. When Jesus said he had come to bring good news to the poor and freedom to the captive, he was saying he had come to affirm the human rights and dignity of people who were oppressed and outcast. This is exactly what we see him doing day after day in the gospels. Sharing bread is sharing love – the giving of a rightful respect to the other person.

The petition in the Lord's Prayer that we should each receive our daily bread is to place the everyday needs of the world within the most profound relationship with God. And to recognize, in the everyday needs of the world, the deep concern of God. In this simple phrase, the ordinary is hallowed. But there is no hallowing without respect and justice.

—◆—

How then can we ourselves pray the words of the Lord's Prayer, 'our bread for tomorrow, give us today', without taking seriously the social justice implications of those words? How can we pray 'give us bread' when our economic and political policies, as a nation and as an international community, ensure that half of our sisters and brothers are imprisoned in degrading and dehumanizing poverty? What does it mean to pray for bread for all of us when our taxation system is so clearly weighted in favour of the wealthy and when our neighbour is denied a secure home to live in and adequate health care and education?

By deluding ourselves and imagining that peace means tranquillity and quietness, we shut ourselves off from the disturbing implications of what Jesus is saying to us – and the challenge that the words of our own most familiar prayer are confronting us with. We withdraw into a religious ghetto of respectable calm and distance ourselves from the concerns of the world outside. But the hands that broke the bread at the Last Supper were human hands. And probably unwashed hands. They were hands which, in a few short hours, would be nailed to the heavy timbers of a cross.

The Lord's Prayer confronts us with the uncomfortable truth that a concern for justice and human rights for our neighbour is a deeply spiritual matter. It is a process by which our awareness and love of God is affirmed or denied. To seek justice in a world blighted by needless suffering and injustice is to engage with the Gospel at its deepest point – to live out the meaning of 'Abba'.

While the Church instinctively wants to stay on the inside, in the false quietness of piety, God is on the outside in the world. The world he loves so much, said St John, that he gave his only Son so we may all have bread. No wonder Jesus referred to himself as the Bread of Life. No wonder they crucified him for daring to reveal God in the sweat and grime of the real world.

The question is: Are we still crucifying him for doing this in our lives? Or do we have the courage and the commitment to say the Lord's Prayer and mean it?

———◆———

Day 28   Week 5
TUESDAY
THE EXTRAVAGANCE OF GOD

Most people do not realize how much time clergy spend in fundraising. Church buildings are expensive to build – and to repair. You can imagine, then, how welcome was the visit from a wealthy member of the congregation who arrived at the minister's house to announce he had had yet another stroke of good fortune. He had come into a very large inheritance.

'I have come to give thanks to God,' he told the minister. 'I want to make a thank-offering.' The minister was not sure what a thank-offering was, but he was soon to find out. The wealthy church member pulled out his cheque book and wrote a cheque for church funds. The minister did not have the discourtesy to look at the amount but thanked his parishioner profusely as he showed him to the door. Returning to his study, he picked up the cheque. It was for £25. The minister did not know whether to laugh or to cry.

Some years ago I went to the funeral of a disturbed young man who had often been homeless. He was a regular visitor to a church centre which had been set up to give support to vulnerable people sleeping rough or otherwise at risk. Philip had eventually been found a flat where, with the help of a social worker, he had been managing to fend for himself. Then one day we heard the terrible news that Philip was dead. There had been a fire in the flat and he had died from his injuries. He was in his early twenties.

At his funeral service a number of people spoke about their friendship with Philip. In his flat they had noticed prayers he had written. Then a care worker, who had been giving him support, told the story of how he and his partner had gone for a meal at Philip's flat. He had three tins of stewed steak in his kitchen cupboard and emptied all three tins of meat into a pan to feed his guests. 'It was all he had in the house,' said the care worker. 'He gave us everything.'

Thinking back on those two events sometimes, I wonder which of those people was closer to the Kingdom – the rich churchgoer or the homeless young man who scratched simple prayers on a scrap of paper with a pencil stub and poured out all three of his tins of stewed steak for his guests?

Many of us still tend to imagine God as an old man with a

beard, but perhaps he is rather more like young Philip. If not in appearance, then certainly in extravagance. Or do we not glimpse the generosity of God in the Gospels, or in the world around us?

The person who wrote Psalm 8 certainly understood the generosity of God: 'Who are we that you should have created us – bothered with us? When I look up at the awesome galaxies of stars in the night sky, I am speechless with wonder at your creation. When I look at the world around me, I am dazed by its splendour.'

And St John, in his great Gospel, picks up the same sense of speechless wonder: 'In the beginning of all this, there was God. And the Word. And the Word was with God; and the Word was God. And the Word was given to us and was with us.' God loved the world so much, says John, that he gave his own self, his own Son. The Bread of Life for all those who will accept him.

When we pray the words 'the bread for tomorrow, give us today' or 'give us today our daily bread', we are not begging God to give us what he would otherwise withhold. We do not have to persuade God to give us life. God is pouring life out for us every second of the day in an extravagance of love.

—◦—

And this generosity is mirrored in the gospels. The wedding at Cana in Galilee, as we have seen, was an exercise in crazy merriment. An act of overwhelming generosity as the hosts went from the humiliating crisis of having no wine at the wedding, to having so much wine that every person in the village could have wine for a week. There is an echo of it in the comment of Jesus that he came eating and drinking and was condemned by the religious leaders as being a glutton and a drunkard. There is even an echo of it in the dark drama of the Last Supper on the night he was betrayed. 'I will not drink of the fruit of the vine with you again until we drink it together in the Kingdom,' he says. There is going to be wine in the Kingdom? Who knows!

The generosity of God finds an echo in those strange miracles when the hungry crowds are fed. Three loaves and two fishes in some bizarre way produce not just enough for thousands of people, they provide too much food. After the meal they collect basket upon basket of left-over scraps from the feast. Why on earth do the gospel writers bother to tell us what happened after the crowds had been fed? Because it is a sign that what has happened is not an exercise in survival, but a banquet. Food for today, but also food for the Great Tomorrow.

And look how Jesus picks up on the generosity of spirit of others. The woman who had lived an immoral life weeps in remorse and pours costly perfume over his feet as he reclines at supper in the home of the mean-spirited cleric. His host protests, but Jesus cuts in with the story of the merciful money-lender: One man owed him 500 silver pieces and another owed him 50. The moneylender cancelled both their debts.

'Which will be the more grateful?' asks Jesus.

'The one who was let off most,' answers his host.

'You are right,' says Jesus, 'and that is why this woman is so happy. Because her sins are forgiven.'

——•——

The life God offers us in his generosity is bread for today and bread for the Great Tomorrow. The woman with the costly perfume knew that; the people sitting on the grass, having just been fed with the loaves and the fishes knew that; the people in the village of Cana knew that. Our friend Philip who asked his care worker to dinner probably knew that.

This is a God who seems to delight in opening all the tins of stewed steak at once. But where that leaves the rich man with the cheque, I do not know.

——•——

Day 29   Week 5
WEDNESDAY
THE FIRST CASUALTY

A friend of ours recently went on a peaceful demonstration march in London. During the event there was small incident in which the police were involved, but otherwise the march passed off uneventfully. She was therefore surprised and annoyed to see the march portrayed on the evening TV news bulletin as a riot. 'What took place on the street bore no relation to the news broadcast,' she said later, and added, 'I will never believe anything I see in a TV news report again.'

Anyone who has worked in the media will testify there is a powerful incentive among editors to sell newspapers and among TV producers to keep their viewer ratings high. And, as in war, the first casualty in the battle for commercial survival can often be the truth. The old adage in journalism that the facts are sacred has increasingly been changed to, 'If the facts don't fit, change them.'

But there are more reasons for changing the facts than spicing up an otherwise flagging news bulletin. Communication is about power. To control information and knowledge, and to be able to influence the way people think and perceive the world, is vitally important if you want to exercise and retain power. Over the last 20 years in Britain, the press has been crucial to the way power has been increasingly concentrated in the hands of the wealthy. One way in which it has succeeded in doing this is by distorting the truth about those who do not have power. Thus, homeless and unemployed people have been systematically condemned in many papers as scroungers, parasites and wasters. Unwilling to work and unable to handle what money they do have.

For those of us with a closer acquaintance with the reality of those people's lives, that is a gross distortion of the truth. And it is an intentional distortion. If we believe people are wilfully homeless and deliberately unemployed, then it is easy to feel free of any responsibility for their situation – blaming the victim is a classic way of dealing with guilt. One of the reasons Jesus was so unpopular with the powerful people of his own day was that he spoke the truth about the poor and the outcast. Perhaps it would be more accurate to say he lived the truth. By befriending them and sharing food with them, he was not being nice to poor people. He was expressing the truth that these people were ordinary, vulnerable human beings, accepted and loved by God.

No wonder he said he was the Way, the Truth and the Life. But how interesting that the Church seems to have concentrated on his being the Way and the Life. The idea that the Christ person is also the truth about God is a less attractive proposition. And yet, in our exploration of the meaning of the words of the Lord's Prayer 'our bread for tomorrow, give us today', the idea of the word of truth is crucially important.

―●―

Of all the homeless people I have been privileged to know, perhaps only one in a hundred has tried to beg money from me. What they have wanted has not been handouts, but honesty. The honesty of being recognized as a human being. There has been a real irony in the fact that, although I went to work in the inner city assuming I was going to minister to the poor, in the event it has been they who by their patience and insight have ministered to me.

I have been fed in my understanding and awareness of God, and in my awareness of myself as a human being of worth, by people who I had assumed had nothing to offer me. How wrong I was. And how amazing to discover that, while I was the one formally ordained by the Church as a minister, God was ministering to me through this 'priesthood of the poor' on the streets of the city.

Suddenly we begin to realize that the idea of 'bread for tomorrow' is not just limited to its place in the Lord's Prayer, but is scattered across the gospels. Again and again in St John's mighty gospel, we hear expressions like: 'I am the Bread of Life; I am the water of life; the [life-giving] teaching that I give is not my own but of the one who sent me; if you dwell in the revelation [truth] that I bring you, then you are my disciples and the truth will set you free . . .'

Given life, given nourishment, set free from fear and from all that imprisons us. That takes us right back to the beginning of the gospel accounts: 'I have been sent to proclaim good news [the truth about God] to the poor, to proclaim release for the prisoners . . .' But good news for the poor and release for the prisoners is not just about food handouts, as we have seen. It is about living out the truth about God and seeking the fulfilment and well-being of all of our neighbours – regardless of religious creed, social class, skin colour or gender.

No wonder Jesus was angry about the plight of the leper who

came and knelt before him, and about all the other people who were degraded and marginalized by the ruling power elite. Part of his anger was at their suffering, but much of it stemmed from the knowledge that their suffering was caused by the untruth of the religious system.

For Jesus to have said he was the Way, the Truth and the Life implies an existing situation which is contrary to the will of God – which is untruthful, which offers a false way forward and which is destructive of life. The Christ person was not crucified for healing people. He was crucified for challenging a system which dehumanized people. A system which was a denial of the Kingdom of God.

The bread for tomorrow involves the truth for today. And people in positions of power do not want the truth to be too readily available.

———◆———

Day 30   Week 5
THURSDAY
SHAKE THE BOTTLE

Today I am ill. It is official – my daughter has admitted it. I went to the chemist's yesterday and came away with a big bag containing paracetamol, vitamin pills, cod liver oil capsules, a bottle of Ribena and a box of tissues. I even thought about buying a thermometer. It is only a cold. But a very heavy cold. There is a lot of it about. They say it is sweeping the country and two days ago it reached me.

As a life-long hypochondriac, I can at least enjoy being ill, even though I am shivery, my throat is sore and my head feels as though it is made of wood. Naturally, I have put on an extra layer of clothing and the central heating has been roaring all day. I shall not go out. They say it is advisable to stay in the warm and take plenty of hot drinks.

Not surprisingly, I did not manage to say my prayers until almost lunch-time, but I am sure the Lord will understand. Actually I did my prayers a bit differently today. Instead of using the prayer book, I got a candle and put it on my desk. Behind it I placed a small icon which was made by some of my homeless friends in the city at a little workshop they go to. The candle flame cast a warm glow on the picture.

As I sat quietly saying my prayers, I thought about the people who had made the icon: sanded the flat piece of wood and pasted the picture on to it. I wondered who it was who had varnished it so it looked as though it came from twelfth-century Patmos and not twenty-first-century Leeds. Perhaps it was Gus – or maybe beloved Danny, before they died. They were people I had known and loved dearly. I wondered whether my other friends had caught the colds that were going around. And, if they had, how they were coping? Some of them live intermittently in hostels while others have their own bedsits – often grim, damp places with peeling wallpaper. And what about those who were on the streets, living rough out there in the rain today?

If they have flu or a heavy cold, where will they sleep and how will they keep warm? They will not have central heating or tissues or hot drinks. Their bones will ache and their heads will hurt like mine. But they will not have an intelligent and loving partner to bully them or a sympathetic cat called Florence to sit on their knee by the fire. And so it is that many of them will die. Some will die of cold, but many more will die from despair – the main cause of death of people sleeping rough in Britain today is suicide.

I wondered whether Jesus ever got colds. If he was human, he must have had something wrong with him, some of the time. When we are well, most of us manage to cope with life. But when we are ill, we just want to curl up in the warm and sleep. But where could he curl up and sleep when he was ill? Reading the gospels, we discover he often stayed with friends. But he also said that, while the birds had their nests and the foxes their holes, the Son of Man had nowhere to lay his head. And often, maybe, no one to make him a hot drink. Jesus was human like me and you and Danny and Gus – and sometimes he needed a place just to be.

Perhaps that is part of the 'give us our daily bread' petition in the Lord's Prayer. We are human in our relationships with other people and, being human, we are vulnerable – sometimes to flu bugs. When we are feeling low we need to be supported and cared for, and maybe God knows that. Perhaps one of the things the prayer is saying is that we all need caring and nourishing. Let us try to care for and nourish each other. Grant that we may receive for tomorrow our daily nourishment.

As I take my next dose of tablets, I think back to what it used to say on the medicine bottles when I was a child: Shake well before use. Why did it say that? So that the bits at the bottom would get mixed in with the liquid at the top. Because it was the stuff which had sunk to the bottom of the bottle that did you the most good.

I think of my friends who are homeless – people with no regular work, no regular income. People who are often ill. These are people at the bottom of the bottle we call society. These are people who have been amazingly kind to me over the years. They have helped me come closer to God – and to be more willing to accept myself, with all my failings. They have spoken words of encouragement, blessing and absolution to me and helped me to understand what it is to be a priest. They have cared for me and nourished me and given me the daily bread of life I have needed. The Church teaches that I am the priest and they are the people. But they have fed me with the Bread of Life.

Jesus said he had come to proclaim good news to the poor. Some of us are receiving the good news *from* the poor.

Maybe, as we move gradually through Lent towards Holy Week, we need to reflect on what God is doing, and how he may be offering us our daily bread. Perhaps we need to have the courage to shake the bottle of society so that some of the people at the bottom come a bit closer to the top. Because, contrary to what many people think, it is the bits at the bottom that do us the most good.

FRIDAY
THREE IS A VERY BIG NUMBER

Once upon a time, when the Church was very young, the Big Angel sent an e-mail to all the Sundays in the year. They were to report to her office at nine o'clock the next morning. 'We need to get things sorted out round here,' she told them when they had assembled. 'And the first thing we are going to do is to give you all names.'

She pointed to a very large Sunday: 'You will be Easter Sunday,' she said. There was a murmur of approval. 'And you will be Pentecost Sunday,' she said to the next Sunday in the group. Going down the list, she handed out names to Mothering Sunday, Palm Sunday, Racial Justice Sunday, Homelessness Sunday, and Advent Sunday. Finally, there was just one Sunday left without a name. 'You are going to be called Trinity Sunday,' she said.

'Trinity Sunday?' they all chorused. 'What on earth is that?' And the newly named Trinity Sunday went pink with embarrassment.

'I thought you'd say that,' said the Big Angel tartly, 'and I have to tell you that it says here on my list that Trinity Sunday is one of the most important Sundays of the year. Now, get out of my office – you make the place look untidy. And don't talk in the corridor,' she shouted after them.

—◆—

Nearly 2,000 years later most people still do not realize that Trinity Sunday is one of the most important Sundays of the year. In fact, most people do not even know what it means. And this has caused a lot of problems.

First of all, Trinity Sunday is about God. Second, it is about the way we experience God. Third, it is a way of making sense of our lives. It is called Trinity Sunday because it is the day we think especially about God. Trinity means three – three particular ways of knowing God. Just like you can have three ways of knowing another person.

Simple example: I have a beloved daughter called Alison. It

seems only yesterday that she was two years old but now she is, apparently, 21 and a qualified physiotherapist. She is also a very wise woman. OK. I relate to Alison in three different ways: First, she is my daughter whom I love dearly; second, she is a physiotherapist who fixed my back when I strained something and could not stand up straight; and third, she is a wise friend to whom I sometimes go for advice. Child, therapist, friend – but she is one person.

Now a not-so-simple example. We can relate to God in three different ways: First, as Abba, Father, the awesome Creator and source of life; second, in the person of Jesus Christ, tangible and recognizable; and, third, as the bond of love that exists between us all – the power and creative force which inspires us to respond to each other as people. Three ways of experiencing God: God above us; God alongside us; God within us. But one God.

So why bother? Why is this important? It is important because, unless we keep a sense of all three aspects of God, we damage our relationship with him and with each other. And this throws the whole of our lives out of balance.

Think about bread again. As we have begun to discover on this Lenten pilgrimage, the Lord's Prayer has hidden depths. It is not just speaking here about the day's shopping – it is speaking about the gift of life itself. Bread for each day as an expression of God's creative love – and bread for us together as people living in community with each other. Bread for today, but bread for all time. There is a trinity process going on.

First, we receive the bread as a life-giving gift from the Father as an act of undeserved grace. Second, we recognize it and internalize it in the physical form of food, both as a loaf of bread and as the Christ person, the Bread of life. In the Eucharist those two merge completely when Jesus says: Take and eat this bread – in sharing in this loaf you are sharing in all that I am. Third, we receive the bread, not selfishly and individually, but acknowledging that we are, together, the children of God. We are united in the Spirit of his love and able to respond in thanksgiving by the inspiration of that love.

There is also a Trinity process going on when it comes to prayer. We pray to God the Father, the ultimate mystery. Second, we pray in companionship with Jesus, our brother, as he has taught us – and in companionship with our neighbour who is also precious to God and held in the Abba love of God. Third, we are motivated and inspired to recognize and give thanks for the gift of life; the gift we receive by the presence of the Spirit within and among us.

The trouble with the Holy Trinity is it is dangerous. What the Trinity process does is to integrate and recognize the truth of God and of our own humanity. We are called to love God with all our heart and to love and seek justice for our neighbour; and to see those two actions as part of the same powerful, life-changing reality.

The Holy Trinity makes our politics and our social action an expression of prayer. The bread which we share and the struggle to see that people have a right to feed themselves, suddenly becomes a holy and sacramental activity at the heart of our relationship with God. An outward and visible sign of the invisible, but real, love of God.

And how do we know this Trinity process is dangerous? Listen to the politicians and the other holders of power. Christians should stick to their Bibles and not dabble in politics, they say. And they say it because they are afraid. They are afraid of the Trinity process which says God is not just the God of the religious, or the churches – but the God of the world. Everything that happens in the world concerns God – and everything that happens either affirms or denies God's Kingdom. Prayer is about love and love is a social activity. All of our actions are either prayer or a denial of prayer. God is in this with us. That is why the politicians get worried.

———◆———

Day 32 Week 5
SATURDAY
GOD ON-LINE

Great Excitement. Like you seldom hear it these days. After weeks of waiting it has finally arrived. They delivered it in two huge boxes and Eve is now the proud owner of a new computer. Not a second-hand, pass-on from a friend, but a brand new all-singing, all-dancing, multi-mega computer from the factory. We heard all about it when Eve came home from college for the weekend and went to her local church. Amid much hugging, she told everyone the news.

Someone had suggested she may be able to use a computer in her studies and, thanks to a friend, it just happened.

Now, as soon as she can find a computer expert at college, she will be able to write her essays on screen and store them on floppy disks. Not only that, her children will be able to access the Internet, and even send e-mails. A recent article in the educational press suggested that a significant dividing line is emerging in children's education, between those who have access to a computer at home and those who do not. Needless to say, those with a computer will be at a huge advantage, educationally and, later, in the employment market.

Not only has the computer arrived, it has also thrown new light on the Lord's Prayer and the petition: 'Our bread for tomorrow, give us today.' The fact that Eve and her children will be able to surf the Internet means they will have access to a huge amount of knowledge and information. They will be nourished by a rich reservoir of learning. They will, if they use it wisely, be fed so they grow in understanding and awareness. The nourishment they receive each day will be bread for tomorrow. Food for the mind, the soul and the imagination which will enrich their lives. But only if they use it.

Meanwhile, there are new developments at Eve's church. A new vicar has been appointed. And already he is discovering that having a church of your own is very different from being a curate.

You have many more responsibilities and much less time for things like reading. He is a wonderfully gifted young priest who loves reading, but he has just realized he is not going to be able to spend as much time studying as he did in the past.

Older heads may nod sympathetically, but the problem is a serious one. If he does not read another book for a year, no one will notice. But if he does not read regularly for the next few years, he will become under-nourished. A gradual process of starvation will have begun. One day, he will realize he does not have anything to say; no new thoughts or insights. Like growing runner beans on the same piece of land and never digging in any manure, the crop will eventually weaken and fail.

The trouble is we still regard reading as a luxury rather than essential to life. We often have the same attitude to events like retreats and quiet days. Even saying our prayers is regarded more as a duty than as a time when we can be fed by God. How exasperated God must get! We have, in libraries, art galleries, bookshops and the Internet, a vast treasure-house of knowledge and learning. If we made a list of all the great books in the world we would never have time to read them all. And most of us do not even make a start. God must wonder what is wrong with us when we spend hundreds of hours watching mindless entertainment on the television, while ignoring all the resources which surround us. We are happy to criticize people for eating junk food or damaging their health by smoking, but how often do we hear people being criticized for not visiting an art gallery or reading a really great novel?

We think about God speaking to us in the silence of a great cathedral or some other impressive place like a mountain top. But what if God is trying to speak to us through our everyday lives – through the computer sitting on my desk; or the one in your home? We may like to preserve our ancient churches with their stained glass windows, but maybe God is already ahead of us: on-line?

Maybe, when we pray the words: Our bread for tomorrow, give us today, we should really be saying, 'Give us the common sense to gratefully receive the bread you have given us and are giving us day by day' in all the richness of the world – and in all the richness of the Bible. 'Give us today our daily bread' does not just apply to loaves of baked bread – it means all those things which feed us.

Perhaps some of us find it hard to acknowledge that we are people worth nourishing and nurturing. Many of us, especially in what are called the caring professions, spend so much time thinking about other people, we forget about caring for ourselves. We forget, or pretend we do not need that sort of nurturing and care. But God has other ideas. Perhaps that is one reason Jesus told us to say the words 'give us' each day our daily bread. It could be he was telling us to look after our own bodies in a responsible, and respectful, way. Otherwise, like many dried-out runner beans, we will be no use to anyone. And no use to God.

St Paul said that our bodies are like temples, but maybe they are more like gardens which need plenty of good nourishment digging in.

The new computer that arrived at the college this week for Eve is a way of making sure that happens. Food for the soul may come electronically in tomorrow's church. The next time she thinks about her friend the Archbishop of Canterbury, she can send him an e-mail. And scan in pictures of the children. Maybe, even, the frog.

———◆———

PASSION SUNDAY
THE GREAT TEMPTATION

Though the years have passed, sometimes when I am alone I sit and think of her. How she came to see us one evening and sat at our kitchen table and drank a glass of wine. Her name was Alison Norris. We did not know that she was dying.

She had come to work in the city, taking up an important church post which promised to open up new and exciting areas of ministry. Moving from a national job in the Methodist Church in London, she was looking for a house to buy. She needed somewhere temporary to stay and had come to look us over. As she sat at the table by the window, we knew we had made a friend for life. She was a stylish and formidably intelligent woman. We could imagine the dinner parties and the conversations we would all have. After finishing her wine and being shown our spare room, she announced that it would do nicely. She would move in on the following Monday.

But on Sunday they phoned to say she would not be coming. She had been rushed into hospital. The cancer was terminal. It took her 18 months to die. During that time she became a beloved friend. Despite her illness, she bought her own house a mile or so away. Instead of sitting quietly and knitting, she redesigned the kitchen, built book cases, had her first grandchild, went on holiday at the family cottage in the north of Scotland, walked on the fells and went skinny-dipping in the cold, green sea.

She seemed indestructible. But she was not. One day, just after 11 in the morning, the phone call came and she was dead. I can still remember the words at the funeral service:

Woman of truth and integrity; woman of wisdom and learning.
Woman of courage and faith. Of fierce and awesome authority.
And of warm, mischievous humour.
Child and mother, youthful grandmother.
Strong friend, companion, partner and lover.
Collector of pebbles, catcher of fish.
Giver of life and giver of laughter. Woman of God.

Afterwards we went our different ways – back to our different lives, but all of us with one question. Why? Why did this glorious woman have to die? Why was someone so deeply committed to God's Kingdom, so meaninglessly destroyed? And just at the moment when a new and important piece of work in God's service was about to begin? Where was God in that? If he cares so much about the world, where was he the day she started to die? We know the arguments about vulnerability – human freedom being the freedom to love and the freedom to be hurt. But sometimes you wonder.

And there have been other times. When different people committed to the service of others, and to the service of God, have died. When opportunities for new life, for healing and for peace seem to have been mindlessly obliterated. When projects working for social justice have collapsed from lack of funding, while millions have been thrown away on extravagant buildings – statements of power and expressions of ego.

There have been times when the power of evil seems overwhelming and you feel exhausted. And the great temptation is to give up and walk away. Maybe that is why Jesus told us to pray that God would be with us in the great temptation. The temptation to despair and to lose faith itself.

Our translations of the Lord's Prayer read 'Do not bring us to the test' or 'Do not lead us into temptation.' But why would a loving God want to lead us into temptation? Why would God plunge us into the testing ordeal? Perhaps the words meant something slightly different then. When the disciples asked Jesus to teach them to pray his way, they were living in an age when the end of the world was believed to be imminent. At any moment the judgement of God might suddenly break in on them. There was a sense that this final, indescribable event would come upon them as the most terrible ordeal. The words may have been a way of praying for God's help in that ordeal – for the strength to remain true to God in that catastrophe.

Whatever it may have meant to them, it does not mean that now. But the prayer is for us also. So what can it mean today? Perhaps it is a recognition of the inevitable. That if we love God with all our heart and we love our neighbour – living out God's love incarnationally and with justice in our political, economic and social activities – then we will be crucified.

We will be opposed by the powerful and the greedy, the selfish and the rich. We will be starved of support and exhausted by the struggle to live the Christ life. Just as he was exhausted by the struggle. And there will be times when we come to our own Garden of Gethsemane and cry out: 'Enough. I give in. Take this cup away from me.'

As they listened to his words, they did not know how soon their own ordeal would come. He seemed indestructible. A man of truth and integrity, of wisdom and learning. A man of courage and faith. Of fierce and awesome authority and warm mischievous humour. Strong friend, companion – perhaps even lover. Collector of misshapen and discarded pebbles, fisher of men. Giver of life, giver of laughter.

Looking down the last few months of his life, with its gathering storm clouds, he gave them a gift. A simple prayer, in rhyming verses, which even they would be able to remember. As he approached his ordeal, he also saw the ordeal they would face if they were true to God's love. Pray that you will always know God is with you when you face the great temptation, he was saying.

He came to their house one evening and drank a glass of wine. They knew that they had made a friend for life. They did not know that he was dying.

MONDAY
WINNING AT ALL COSTS

Without realizing it, over the past few years, we have all become competitors. We compete for jobs, for university places, for attention, for promotion, for status and for power. The people who are most admired are usually those who have competed most successfully – Olympic gold medal winners, heads of multinational corporations, the prime minister. Those who are least admired tend to be those who have done less well in the competition of life – the unemployed, the homeless, the mentally ill, the poor. One of the few things for which we do not have to compete is the love of God. This comes as an unconditional gift. And yet, even in a religion which celebrates this gift, we find strong competition.

Almost imperceptibly in the last 24 hours we have slipped into that part of the Church's year which is called Passiontide. Passion in this context means 'suffering' and this little-known season is the time when we focus on the suffering of Christ as he approached his death. When he was put on trial and executed. It is a time when we reflect on the willingness of Christ to suffer in order to share with us a new understanding of God's love and the hope this love signifies.

Perhaps it is a natural response to the boundlessness of this gift that the Church has been tempted to express its understanding of the Christ event in absolute terms. This may partly explain the way in which, for example, it describes Jesus Christ as the 'perfect' man and his mother, Mary, as a 'pure' virgin. It is also tempting to see the death of Christ on the cross as total and incomparable human suffering.

Completeness and perfection are attributes of God – and, by association, are attributed to the actions and purposes of God in the world. However, it seems self-evident that the Christ was not perfect in every respect. Presumably he was limited by his own age and he did not have complete knowledge. It seems undeniable that he did not know how computers work, or where America was. Either that or he was not human. And the Church insists he was fully human.

Similarly, references to his sisters and brothers indicate his mother was not permanently a virgin, regardless of the manner of his own birth. So, too, when it comes to the suffering of Christ. We may be fairly certain the modern advances in torture techniques have ensured that political prisoners in the twenty-first century are made to suffer far more, physically and possibly psychologically, than a first-century political prisoner tried and condemned to death in a hurried show trial.

It may be, because of his great love for the world, that Christ did in fact suffer more than any other human being. But what has a league table of suffering got to do with the meaning of the Crucifixion or the love of God? How do such questions arise?

The answer seems to be that they arise out of an instinctive temptation for organizations and groups to be pre-eminent. To compete. This is partly, no doubt, to emphasize their importance – but it is also to emphasize their distinctiveness. This tendency can express itself in particularly malevolent forms of drainpipe theology – and it goes back a long way.

As we have seen, there was a very powerful instinct among the early Hebrews to assert their distinctiveness as a social and religious group, as well as their pre-eminence with God. We have only to read the blood-stained chapters of the Old Testament book of Deuteronomy to be plunged into accounts of ethnic cleansing and genocide. The Hebrews not only saw themselves as 'the' chosen people of God being led to their divinely ordained promised land, but also believed the original inhabitants of the region could be massacred in God's name. Men, women and children.

One of the most terrible, and little known, words in the human vocabulary is the word 'ban'. A ban means the total extermination of a community. People, animals and buildings. Try reading some of the psalms if you are unconvinced. So much for the love of God for the people of Canaan.

The reason for this bloodshed was to affirm the Hebrews' unique relationship with God. They knew this relationship had not come about by their own worth or strength in open competition. They were winners by the gift of God. But, in the years to come, they would fight to retain this competitive pre-eminence.

Centuries later the Church was to be drawn into this same temptation. In the period after Christ's death, we see his followers forming themselves into a distinct group. Distinct from other religious groups. It is not a coincidence that there are significant expressions of anti-Semitism in some of the documents of the early Church. Being, itself, a Jewish church in its early years, it fought to distance itself ideologically from the non-Christian Jewish community from which it had emerged. Just as the Hebrews had fought to distance themselves from their Canaanite neighbours years before.

It is both tragic and ironic that, in the last century, the extermination of millions of Jewish people in Europe has mirrored this ghastly process. The Nazis, convinced they were the master race and competitively supreme, sought to exterminate the Jewish people in their own territories. But this act of barbarism has, in turn, created a further mirror effect.

Since the end of the Second World War, the Jewish people's own identity has been closely tied up with this event. They have tended to believe that they alone have experienced the ultimate in human suffering; such that their identity is in danger of being defined by the Holocaust.

Just as the Church has been tempted to 'hoard' to itself the importance and totality of Christ's suffering, so the Jewish community has tended to do the same with the Holocaust experience. The decision to establish an international Holocaust Day of Remembrance met with unease within the Jewish community itself and a warning from some Jewish people that they should not take over and possess the totality of suffering of those years. Polish people, gypsies, homosexuals and many others also perished in the Holocaust.

In the last few years, it has been pointed out, the ethnic cleansing carried out by the Nazis against Jewish people and others has been mirrored, to a lesser degree, by the state of Israel in its hostility to its Palestinian neighbours – not least, in its determination to build Israeli housing settlements on Palestinian land.

It could be further argued that both Jewish people and gentiles have been equally indifferent to the massive suffering caused by the political and economic interests of big business since the two great wars. More people die, day by day, because of the food marketing strategies of some business corporations than ever died in the Holocaust. Are these people of different worth as well as people of different skin colour? There is an argument which holds that, since the Holocaust was carried out as the official policy by an elected government, it is therefore without parallel in human conduct. However, this important distinction may be of little comfort to a mother nursing her starving child because of the less official policies of private companies.

Temptation comes in many forms. One of the most pernicious is the temptation to claim religious supremacy under the guise of being true to the love of God. The commandment which Christ chose to sum up the will of God was the command to love, not the command to be right. He chose to live alongside those who were believed to have been consistently wrong in most of the things they had done, and to be failures in the great competition of life.

Reflecting on our Lenten pilgrimage on the passion of Christ, we need to ensure we do not add to that suffering by our own arrogance and the temptation to compete. 'I am among you as one who serves,' he told them. 'Go and do likewise.'

Day 35   Week 6
TUESDAY
ROBIN HOOD THEOLOGY

It is many years since Robin Hood figured significantly in my life. However, happy childhood memories of the TV adventures of the hero of Sherwood Forest were rekindled a few days ago when I met someone who goes to the church where Robin Hood and Maid Marion are said to have married. Whether or not the legend is true, many people come to visit Barbara's church at Edwinstowe in Nottinghamshire.

The real Robin Hood is lost in the mists of time, but the legend of his daring deeds and his constant battles to oppose injustice lives on. I can still remember the song about him robbing the rich to feed the poor.

As we move through the last weeks of our Lenten pilgrimage and reflect on the words of the Lord's Prayer, 'Lead us not into temptation but deliver us from evil', we could do worse than pause for a minute to think about Robin Hood and the meaning of temptation.

─◆─

Temptation and evil are bound up with the idea of sin and, if we want to unravel the meaning of the Lord's Prayer, we need to be clear what we mean by sin. Unfortunately, the Church has been less than helpful on some occasions. Not unnaturally, it has used the scriptures for guidance. However, the Bible is not a homogeneous book. It contains many different documents, written in different situations, which give very different messages, as we have discovered.

In the early part of the Bible we see, in some parts of the Old Testament, a strong identification with sin as the breaking of the law. It has been politically expedient over the years for power groups to continue this association of sin and law-breaking. However, as we have come to realize, Christ himself broke the religious law – from which it was said that nothing must be added or taken away. Instead he added and took away. But how could this be, when the law was the law of God? Jesus was believed, even by his enemies, to be a religious teacher. How could this person deliberately do things which, in the eyes of their inherited law, were sinful?

The answer seems to be in the words of the Christ himself. Instead of laying down a large and complex set of negative and restrictive rules, he gave his followers a positive law. To love. To love God and to love all and every neighbour. But love is about relationship – and relationship is the key to both our understanding of sin, and our understanding of God.

Let us see how this works out in practice. It says very clearly in the Old Testament that it is a sin to steal – to take what legally belongs to another person. So did Robin Hood sin when he stole from the rich to give to the poor?

Operating on the understanding of sin which we find in some parts of the Old Testament, we might well say that he did. But, obeying Christ's law of love, we could argue the opposite. In stealing from those whose greed condemned the poor to suffering, we could argue that Robin Hood was fulfilling Christ's commandment to love his neighbour. If we accept the possibility that the love of God may be unconditional and that God loves the greedy rich and the hungry poor, then how can we reflect that love in an unjust situation? It may be we do this by taking what the rich have hoarded and sharing it with the poor.

The fact that Robin Hood lived nearly 1,000 years ago gives us a reassuring sense of distance in this gentle debate. However, the principle still confronts us today. In Southern Africa, over the past 400 years, millions of black people have been forcibly removed from their homes and land, and then dumped in arid wasteland areas called homelands. Since the end of apartheid, South Africa has gone through a process of 'truth and reconciliation'. The truth of the greed and violence of the apartheid system has been exposed – and there has been a call to forgiveness and reconciliation.

But the question arose: Could there be real truth and reconciliation without reparation, without the whites returning the stolen land to its black owners? Some of the land, which had been appropriated in the mid-twentieth century was still legally owned by the former black residents – they still held the legal title. But, for millions of others, there was no legal right and, like the indigenous American Indians and the Australian Aboriginal people, they had no way of claiming what had been taken from them.

What applies to property also applies to sex. And, surprisingly, there is a connection between the two. The connection is power and control. Land gives power and wealth. Power and wealth provide the levers for control. Control ensures that power and wealth remain in the hands of the dominant group. So what about sex?

Sexual behaviour is a primary factor in human relationships. But codes of sexual conduct and rules regulating what is clean and unclean/pure and impure are also primary factors in cultural identity – as well as cultural control. We have seen how the ancient Hebrews were convinced of their unique calling as the 'chosen people' of God and the subsequent need to honour this calling by remaining faithful and distinct as a holy nation.

One way in which this distinctiveness was lived out was by a strict code of purity. Only the best was good enough for God; only the pure was the best. Animals for sacrifice therefore had to be without physical blemish and the people had to adhere to a strict code of physical cleanliness. Hands must be washed before meals and particular materials were designated as being unclean. Pork was unclean, for example, as were both semen and menstrual fluid. Materials must not be mixed – there were to be separate dishes for different foods. Neither must roles be mixed, hence the strict control on the role of women.

The human body was almost a symbol of human society. Physical bodily boundaries reflected the importance of national boundaries in a nation which saw itself as a community created by God. Marriage restrictions between Hebrews and gentiles were an example of the need for human and national distinctiveness and purity. Personal and racial purity. Such imperatives were enshrined in the law. The law was believed to be the will of God. Sexual and physical purity was therefore seen as an expression of loyalty to God. And the ruling clergy held the rule book. They interpreted the law and exerted enormous power and control.

Then came Jesus, the Christ. He did not wash his hands before meals. He sat down to eat with people who were clearly unclean in the eyes of the law, both physically and sexually. He frequently and deliberately broke the law of the Sabbath and was willing to become physically defiled in his contacts with the diseased leper and other outcasts.

In breaking the purity laws, he was affirming a higher law – the law of love. This holds that we seek the life and well-being of the other person as an expression of God's own creative and freely given love. Thus to touch the leper was to break the written law, but to affirm the life-giving law of God's love. By the free and inclusive nature of his relationships, and the way in which he repeatedly crossed cultural boundaries, he jeopardized the distinctive nature of his own people. And threatened the power and control the ruling group exercised. No wonder he had to die.

But he also threatens some of our own securities and assumptions. What happens to our traditional ideas of sinfulness if the most life-giving opportunity for a homeless young person is to be fostered by an adult who is a lesbian? Many people have been brought up in the Church to believe that single gender sexuality is always sinful. It is a mixing of the traditional pattern of human behaviour – it is characteristically a Canaanite and not a Hebrew custom. But the Hebrews believed it was right to exterminate political opponents, women and children included. Where are we being led?

Perhaps we are being led by Christ to ask: What is the most life-giving course of action in any situation? If God allowed his own Son to come into the world so that we might have life, should we ourselves not seek in every situation to affirm that life? Sin may not be so much to do with breaking a written law as much as breaking or damaging our relationship of love with God and with our neighbour.

Maybe that is why my beloved friend Aidan is such a good priest and why his homosexuality may not be a sin but a part of God's gift of life. But to admit that may mean letting go of some deeply held assumptions, and letting go of some of our power. Crossing boundaries – finding life.

WEDNESDAY
THE BIG FISHERMAN

It was a beautiful summer's day. Out on the lawns of the conference centre, some teenagers were throwing a frisbee to each other
– chasing the plastic disc as it spun through the air. With them
was a much older man with a red face and large ears. He was
wearing an old black pullover, which gave him the appearance of
a weathered trawler fisherman. They were having a great time in
the sun.

Meanwhile around the edge of the lawns stood the other conference participants, taking their afternoon tea-break. Among them
were a number of bishops, immaculate in their purple clerical shirts
and those light-coloured linen jackets that constitute summer
uniform for many senior clergy. Finally, it was time for the next
conference session and the youngsters on the lawn ended their
rowdy game. It was only then that we realized who the old fisherman
in the shapeless black pullover was. Cardinal Basil Hume.

The following day something embarrassing happened. The
delegates at the conference came from different Christian denom-
inations: Anglican, Baptist, Methodist, Catholic and others. We had
met in the chapel for an Anglican communion service conducted
by the Archbishop of Canterbury. In the congregation was Basil
Hume.

As the time drew near for the distribution of the bread and
wine, it became clear that, being a Catholic, Cardinal Hume
would not be permitted to receive Communion. He would have to
stay in his seat. A number of people were alarmed, therefore, to see
him stand and quietly walk to the front with the others who were
receiving Communion. How could he break the rules of his own
church?

As he stood in front of the Anglican Archbishop, who was
distributing the Communion bread, Basil Hume bowed his head
to receive a blessing. Then the big fisherman went back to his seat.

When we pray 'Lead us not into temptation but deliver us from
evil', we are actually asking God to help us to resist a tendency

which is basic to our human nature – or perhaps to our animal nature. For millions of years, animals and humans have survived by competing with each other for food and territory. They have instinctively sought security and survival, with the dominant members of the herd or the tribe succeeding. No doubt some bishops have reached that position by virtue of their inherent holiness; perhaps others have achieved pre-eminence by a more competitive process.

The strange thing about Basil Hume was that he could be incredibly ordinary and incredibly holy at the same time. A deeply spiritual person, he once gave an amazing radio interview when Kevin Keegan resigned as manager of Newcastle United. Basil Hume was a Newcastle supporter. 'How long have you supported Newcastle?' he was asked. 'Sixty years,' he replied. But that very ordinary and endearing interview did not in any way detract from the deep respect in which Basil Hume was held as a spiritual leader. When he died, he was mourned by millions of people who were neither Catholic nor Christian. Basil Hume seemed to have been able to resist the temptation to compete and to succeed. He was not, it seems, infected by the sin of pride which causes so much damage in the Church and in secular society.

In his own quiet and deep way he was showing people how the Christ life should be lived. Had Christ been at that conference, where would he have been during the tea break? Standing talking to the dignified bishops; or cavorting round the lawn with a bunch of teenagers, throwing a frisbee and generally getting hot and sweaty? The answer is we do not know – and that probably does not matter. Except there is an important dynamic working here.

—•—

Right from our first encounter with Jesus in the wilderness experience, we see him resisting the temptation to grasp at power. He rejects the temptation to manipulate God by putting him to the test – and the temptation to go for political power in his own nation. Instead he chooses to remain vulnerable.

In his encounters with ordinary people, there is a repeated call for him to set himself up as a political leader. The crowds see in him a champion for their cause – someone who might be able to lead an uprising against the Roman army of occupation. But repeatedly Jesus rejects this pressure. Quite the reverse – he is often seen telling people not to even speak of what he is saying and doing. Why should there be this secrecy about his work?

One explanation is that he saw how essential it was to remain free of political entanglement. That meant resisting the temptation to grasp at power and control. And that is true for us. Too often the Church has been guilty of the idolatry of power and has, in its own conduct, been a source of bondage and oppression to others. We need to resist the temptation to dominate and control and to reject the lure of claiming for ourselves the sovereignty which belongs to God. May your Kingdom come, your will be done.

We need to be guided by the Jesus model. Repeatedly, we see him pointing away from himself and directing people to respond to God. His chosen role was one of servanthood, not dominance. At the Last Supper, the last meal he shared with his disciples before his arrest and execution, he kneels to wash their feet – just as a slave would kneel to wash the feet of house guests. He could have demanded that the disciples kneel to wash his feet; indeed, Peter protests that this is what should be happening.

The whole of the Christ event is, however, a living out of a very radical truth – that we receive life when we are prepared to risk losing it. Love is about giving, but it is in such giving that we receive. And we shall see that lived out in the events of the cross and Resurrection – to which our journey is inexorably leading us.

–◆–

THURSDAY
THE ACCEPTABLE FACE OF EVIL

Today the papers are full of it. An elderly woman was beaten to death by two youths who broke into her home. Now they have been convicted of her murder. It was a senseless act of brutality and the press are making the most of it. 'These Evil Monsters' say the banner headlines in this morning's paper. Not long ago another elderly person in the city was kicked to death. He had been sleeping rough in a shop doorway. A gang of young drinkers, coming out of one of the many pubs in the city centre, saw him and thought it would be good fun to give him a kicking. So they did. And he died. Asleep and alone; harming no one, he was kicked to death. His attackers have not been found. Their evil goes unpunished.

But why do we call such acts of violence evil? What does evil mean? Is it something that infects people, or are they born evil? Can we say a person is evil or do they commit acts which we declare to be evil? A few days ago, reflecting on the death of Alison Norris, we found ourselves talking about the power of evil. Is there such a power or is that just a figure of speech for what cannot be described?

In the past, people have personified evil in the form of the devil or Satan. We all know the pictures of the little monster with the horns and the forked tail carrying a trident. In the gospels, Jesus is pictured as being tempted by Satan – confronted by the presence of evil in a tangible form. Christians differ on whether that was an image which had meaning in that far-off age, or whether it is still a reality today.

What we can say is that there are actions which are so destructive and seemingly senseless, we call them evil. And what we seem to be saying is that these actions are, by their consequences and by their nature, destructive of life – and of life-giving relationships. They go against the will and purpose of God as we see them revealed in the person of Jesus. They are, in a way, acts of rebellion against God and acts of destruction against the life-giving process which he seems to have willed for us. Evil seems to be the exact opposite of love – the exact opposite of creative God-given life.

The elderly man asleep in the shop doorway was not valued and respected by his fellow citizens. But he was precious to God, and God's will for him was that he should have life in all its generous fullness. Instead he was kicked to death and God's will for him was denied.

Our instinctive reaction is one of condemnation. These evil monsters, the papers say. And so do we. And it may be these people are evil. But we ourselves are evil also. We do not kick elderly people to death but we, too, rebel against the life-giving love of God in a thousand different ways. And suddenly we are using that word again – we.

It is an acknowledgement that we are not loved by God in isolation – that we do not live in isolation. We live in society; in relationship with each other. In community. One person's death diminishes all of us. And often we share in the responsibility for that death. Just as drainpipe theology encourages the idea that we can have a private and individual relationship with God, so the idea of sin has also been personalized until we think of it almost exclusively in individualistic terms. But if we live in community with each other and our humanity is influenced, if not determined, by our relationships with each other, then perhaps we should start to think a little more about the idea of corporate sinfulness and corporate evil. Evil for which we carry a shared responsibility.

But we do not simply relate to each other in single-layer human groupings. We also build structures of organization and power. We create commercial companies, international churches, political parties, governments and independent nation states. We help to create these structures, and we have a shared responsibility for their actions. Just as we can speak of an individual being evil or sinful, so too we should recognize that there is such a thing as structural evil and sinfulness.

This does not necessarily mean we can say that an organization is evil, but it does mean we can say the actions of an organization, whether commercial or political, can be evil in their intent and their consequences. Looking back on the history of the Christian Church and the many nation states that have come and gone over the years, it seems we can identify policies and actions which are against the will and desire of God that we should all have life.

And why is this so important? Because, when we realize we have both a personal and corporate responsibility to each other, we discover the invitation from God to receive the gift of life is one which has both personal and corporate implications. Once more we discover God is not some sort of religious relic locked away in a church building, but that he is the God of the whole world – calling us to life. Immediately our faith becomes a matter not just for Sunday worship but also for our weekday lives. Our politics and our economic decisions then become matters integral to our faith. Our bank book becomes as holy as our prayer book. Or as sinful and hypocritical. How can we say we love God and our neighbour when the neighbour whom God loves is homeless on the streets of a wealthy city, and millions of God's children across the world live in degrading poverty and die needlessly because of our greed?

It was not by chance that St John said God loves the world. Our problem is finding the courage to take that truth seriously – to confront evil in all its forms; to realize that evil may be something we have been colluding with all our lives as we silently contribute to the deprivation and death of others. Monsters we may not be, but sinful we most certainly are. Thank God that Jesus, the Christ person, said he had come to bring hope to such as us.

———◆———

Day 38   Week 6
FRIDAY
THOSE EMPTY STREETS

The streets were quiet in the early morning rain. A slow milk-float was the only sign of life as I parked outside the city-centre church. It was just after seven o'clock and hardly light. The wind seemed bitter, as though the absence of pedestrians lowered the temperature. Perhaps the city crowds act as a wind-break. Do people make a city warmer?

As I headed off towards the railway station, I noticed the bin bag in the lane at the side of the church. I looked again and saw it was the huddled figure of a young man. He sat motionless on the deserted pavement, his head bowed on his chest. It was no place to be begging – or sleeping. I looked at my watch. The train went in a few minutes and there was no time to stop.

It was warm on the train and the rain was driven in horizontal streams across the carriage window as we powered through Doncaster on the way to London. The ticket inspector came and went. I thought of the huddled figure on the pavement. Perhaps he was waiting for the church café to open. Perhaps he was out of it on drugs. Perhaps he was dead. I thought of the fact that people living rough on the streets are usually dead by the age of 42 and that the most common cause of those deaths is suicide. Perhaps Nick, the vicar, would see him when he arrived to open up. Nick always seemed to have time for people.

I thought about other young men and women who would be on the streets that day selling the *Big Issue* magazine. They would have a hard time of it. They would keep their magazines in a plastic bag to stop them getting soaked by the rain, but while the magazines would remain dry, they themselves would be cold and wet.

I remembered a city-centre 'retreat on the streets' we had run some weeks before. A young student was among those who had spent a day alone on the streets, reflecting on the love of God for the city and its people. She had fallen into conversation with a *Big Issue* seller who told her he had only managed to sell three magazines that morning. Doubtful about his story she agreed to take a handful of magazines and stand on the opposite side of the street to see how many she could sell.

Two hours later she was in tears. She had sold one magazine and had watched her friend across the street doing little better. Later she told us about the deep sense of rejection she had felt as hundreds of people walked past without a glance. She had always assumed the stories of *Big Issue* sellers making a fortune each day were true. While her friend had remained apparently calm in the face of his rejection, she had felt an increasing anger as people walked past unheeding. Or perhaps he dealt with his pain and anger in other ways.

Reflecting on her experience, the young student realized she had been deeply shocked, not just by the lack of generosity of the people of the city as they strode past on their purposeful journeys, but at their apparent complacency. It was not that they seemed to be guiltily avoiding eye contact and walking past on the other side, but that they seemed totally oblivious to her. She was being rejected not as the seller of a magazine, but as a person. It was as though she did not exist.

Talking this over, we wondered whether this was partly to do with the effects of television and how easy it was becoming to confuse fantasy and reality. Even genuine TV documentaries have an increasingly anaesthetic effect as people mentally switch off to the reality of what is being portrayed. But perhaps it is wrong to blame television for something which is our responsibility. If television is increasingly a form of escapism, then it is we who are tacitly choosing to escape. To deny our calling to be human. Lead us not into temptation.

◄●►

Perhaps Christ experienced the same process. The crowds came to hear him speak and lined the streets with their cloaks as he entered the city. But what was really happening? Was this celebrity event an escape from the boredom of their daily lives? There is a phrase which Jesus used that gives us an indication of what may have been happening. And it may reveal his own anger at the complacency and lack of engagement with reality of the people around him.

The crowds flocked to him. They followed him. Or did they? Do you really want to be a follower of mine? he asked them. Then you must leave your own self behind and take up your cross and follow me. You must be willing to let go of that which is dearest to you – whatever gives you most security and worth. You must risk and be willing to embrace your own death – for the cross was a grotesquely real symbol of a terrible form of execution.

'Take up your cross.' Perhaps he is also saying that to us. And to me. Just what was so vitally important about catching that train? Was it the security of needing to be in London on time or the comfortable cloak of professionalism with which I travelled in that warm carriage? Only a few weeks before we had reflected on the complacency of all the people who had walked past that young *Big Issue* seller and his unofficial apprentice. Was that really so much worse than walking past a bin bag abandoned in a rainy street?

Day 39   Week 6
SATURDAY
COLLISION COURSE WITH DEATH

The tragedy of the sinking of the Titanic has enthralled generations for almost a century. It is partly because the liner was the greatest ever built; partly because it was on its maiden voyage carrying millionaires and celebrities; and partly because they had no inkling of the fate that awaited them out on the calm and icy waters of the northern Atlantic that night in 1912. There must have been a moment when the lookout saw the iceberg ahead and frantically signalled a warning to the bridge. But it was too late.

Inexorably the liner ploughed into the huge iceberg and the ship they claimed was unsinkable was doomed. Aboard the liner, it is said, the passengers hardly felt the impact as the enormous cliff of ice ripped a fatal wound down the side of the ship's gleaming hull and the water started to pour in. For days the ship had been steaming towards the iceberg – and the iceberg had been slowly drifting towards its rendezvous with the Titanic. Both were on a collision course with death. Somewhere in that process there came a moment in time when it was too late to prevent the tragedy and more than a thousand people were already dead.

There comes a time in our journey through Lent when we reach that same moment. And we have reached it now. Tomorrow the crowds will welcome Jesus the Christ into the city with shouts of encouragement and delight. They will throw their cloaks down to make a carpet for him. It will be a time of celebration. Few of them will have an inkling of the fate which awaits this young man as he rides into the city. Few of them will be aware of the fatal collision course he is on – and which he has chosen to accept.

The risk-taker, the law-breaker, the pain-sharer is now also the sin-bearer. In the Communion service we hear the words: 'Jesus, bearer of our sins, have mercy on us.' And, standing at the altar, I think of all my sins which I cannot bear to contemplate and I wonder how this young person half my age can bear them. Mine and the sins of the world. But how can he bear my sin? How can a mother bear the pain of her child who is diagnosed with cancer? How can a lover bear the pain of a dying companion and partner? How can we bear the pain of another person? By being open and vulnerable so we share in their suffering.

But sin means more than suffering. It means the tearing apart of a relationship – a breaking of trust and a denial of love. As Jesus moves nearer to his death, he knows he is holding together the love of God and the rejection of the world. And that seemingly impossible task will soon tear him apart. Looking down from a hillside at the city below, Jesus cries out in anguish: 'How I longed to gather your children as a hen gathers her brood under her wings. But you would not let me.'

Teaching, healing, ministering and sharing the unconditional love of God, Jesus is open and vulnerable. Vulnerable to the incoming anger and hatred of the sin of the world. The religious authorities are silently moving into position and preparing for the kill. The target is coming quietly into range. But, out there, no one seems to be aware of what is happening.

No one, except a woman with the small, but very expensive, jar of perfumed oil. Jesus is sitting at table in the house of Simon the leper when the unnamed woman approaches and silently begins to pour the fragrant oil from the tiny bottle onto his head. It is a loving gesture, heavy with symbolism and meaning and financial implications. The other guests, including the disciples, are angry at what they see as the waste – St Mark says they turned on the woman in fury. 'This expensive oil could have been sold and the money given to the poor,' they say. But, unexpectedly, Jesus takes the woman's side and makes a profound statement: 'You will always have the poor among you, but you will not always have me. She has done a fine thing – she has anointed my body for burial.'

He knows the end is near. He is looking death in the face. The enemy is close and the moment has almost come. It comes now, from the most unexpected quarter – from among his own disciples. The gospel accounts differ and John has a significantly different view of the events, so we cannot be absolutely certain what happened next. But, in the gospels of both Matthew and Mark, the sequence of events is clear – Jesus speaks the words of gratitude and approval: This woman has poured out her love and, by honouring me in this way and at such great cost, she has done what none of you realize needs to happen. The anointing of my body for burial.

He is in a lonely place; a wilderness place. Perhaps in that moment Jesus, the Christ person, needs it to happen. In the anguish of his coming death, perhaps he needs a human being to touch him, physically and bodily, with love. The woman touches him with love and with sadness. The fragrance of the oil and the symbolism of her courageous and determined action fill the whole house.

Then it happens. Judas gets up from the table and goes out. Something in him has snapped. He leaves the supper party and goes to the religious leaders. One of Jesus' closest friends is about to betray him. The iceberg has hit. The dying has started. But in the dining rooms aboard the Titanic no one is aware of what has happened. The band plays on, the wine flows freely. A slight tremor but nothing more. It is forgotten in an instant. So, too, at table at the house of Simon, the conversation continues. Only one person is missing and few other people realize what has happened.

I have been anointed to bring good news to the poor, he said. And this woman has anointed my body for my dying. The Titanic's fate was sealed the moment she set her course on that maiden voyage across the north Atlantic. Jesus' fate was sealed the moment he spoke those words of unconditional love for the poor. All that remained was the working out of that dying.

Day 40   Week 7
HOLY WEEK: PALM SUNDAY
BREATHE FORGIVENESS OVER US

In the last 24 hours we have moved into the final phase of our journey. We are no longer pilgrims but participants in an unfolding process of destruction. In our meditations on the Lord's Prayer, we have seen the living out of that first definitive word: Abba, dearest Father. Creator, lover, strong mother, companion, friend. All that God is, we have tried to glimpse and touch. Now, in the final part of understanding the meaning of that powerful Abba concept, we move from cause to effect and come to one of the most important words in the human vocabulary. Forgiveness. The Lord's Prayer, as we are well aware, does not end with the petition about forgiveness. But our journey, and Christ's journey, does. And what need there is for that forgiveness.

Jesus said to the men in the boat: 'Follow me and I will make you fishers of men.' But Jesus was not the only one interested in going fishing. The devil also has souls to catch. Like me, you may have problems recognizing the existence of the devil, but let's just for the moment assume he does exist. How might he operate?

Rather like an angler, I suspect. The pool is approached stealthily. The time chosen is when the fish are feeding. The hook is baited with a tasty-looking artificial fly. The line flicks out and the fly drops delicately onto the surface of the water with hardly a ripple, right in front of the fish. The fish seems to hesitate, then takes the bait and is hooked. It struggles, but that only drives the barbed hook deeper into its flesh.

Sin operates in just this way. Quietly and cleverly, the devil offers us the bait of something seemingly good. Jesus, my friend, you are hungry. Turn this stone into bread. Jesus, my friend, you are gifted. Why not use that gift? You can have the whole world for your possession. Jesus, my friend, see how God loves you. Take him at his word – throw yourself down from this pinnacle and watch how he will send his angels to catch you.

Each temptation probes for a weakness and the third temptation is aimed at the very heart of Jesus' relationship with his father. We have only to read the words of Psalm 91 to glimpse where this attack is coming from and why it is so penetrating. The psalm is the most amazing symphony of love and trust. The opening movement is quiet and restrained: 'You that live under the shelter of the Most High and lodge under the shadow of the Almighty... he will cover you with his pinions and you shall find safety beneath his wings.'

But then the psalm moves into a triumphant and exultant peon of praise: 'You shall not fear the hunters' trap by night or the arrow that flies by day. A thousand may fall at your side and ten thousand close at hand... but you it shall not touch. For he has charged his angels to guard you in all your ways.'

Then the psalm reached its deepest point: 'Because he cleaves to me in love, I will deliver him. I will protect him because he knows my name...'

Normally, the word 'cleave' means to separate but, here, it means exactly the opposite. To cleave is to press against and adhere to; to bond with and to become inseparable from. To become one. This is the essence of the Christ person's relationship with the Father. There is an indissoluble bond of love. The Son holds to, and is bonded with, the Father. This is the essential relationship which the tempter seeks to penetrate and destroy.

Jesus, my friend, prove that the Father and you are one – that you cleave to Him in love. Does it not say in this, your favourite psalm, that he has charged his angels to protect you?

But that was years ago in the desert. Now we are in the city and it is almost finished. There is anxiety – perhaps fear of what may lie ahead. Is it really necessary to take things to their bitter end, and to take the disciples with him into the abyss?

Jesus, my friend, you have done enough. You are tired. You have succeeded. You have shown the world the meaning of God's love. You have lived out his love for the poor and the rejected. You have courageously opposed the rich and the powerful. You have fought for justice. But there is no need to actually die. What would that prove? It is so crude. So obvious. So gauche. So un-Anglican. God can do all things. Let him take this cup of needless suffering from you.

Peter, how brave you are. You have come right into the court-yard of the High Priest to be close to your Lord. What courage. Sit and warm yourself by this fire. What harm in that, my friend?

Are you not a friend of his? a serving maid suddenly asks.

Who, me? No. Not me. I do not know him, says Peter. Caught off guard, he deflects the challenge. A moment of embarrassment, but no harm done. But the serving maid is perplexed. I think he is one of them, she says to a bystander. Danger suddenly looms. I am not his friend, says Peter.

Then the proof. You are one of them, says somebody in the gathering crowd. You are a Galilean. You speak like he speaks. You have the same northern dialect. You are his friend.

Peter panics. Cursing and swearing in his fear and anger, he shouts the terrible words of denial: 'I do not know this man!' His angry cry echoes across the courtyard, perhaps into the rooms of the High Priest. A cock crows. The hook sinks deep. A man turns in sadness towards the sound of his friend's voice. And Peter dies.

—•—

If sins carried a health warning, maybe we would not get trapped by them so easily. But they do not. They come wrapped in inno-cence and flavoured with goodness. How many affairs begin with a simple friendship? The good companionship of someone who makes the sky seem bluer; the grass greener; the air smell sweeter. Someone who makes you feel more alive. What can possibly be wrong with such a friendship?

How many wars begin with patriotism and loyalty? My King and my Country. The defence of the realm. Our heritage; our England. How many divisions in the Church have begun with a sincere concern for truth? With a genuine desire to discern the will of God. To give due recognition to the authority of the Bible, or parts of it. And suddenly we are burning our sisters and brothers at the stake. How many people, whether in church or state, began by wanting nothing more than to serve others, yet end up destroy-ing them?

'The worst sin is pride, not sex,' says the Church. And it is right, but it never says why. At theological college they told us we had to say Morning and Evening Prayer every day. But they did not tell us why. And I could not see the point. I thought I knew better. So I did not say my prayers. And seven years later I fell apart. I did not know that Morning and Evening Prayer were a life-support system keeping me nourished and attentive to God. I thought I was saving time. I learned the hard way and came to repent of that particular sin, as well as others which came wrapped in innocence and flavoured with goodness.

Some carry the scars of wounds got courageously. Others carry the scars of self-inflicted injury and they are harder to bear. Jesus, the Christ person, carries the first sort in hands and feet. Me and Peter carry the other sort, as do many people in this world. Father, forgive.

<hr />

Day 41   Week 7

HOLY WEEK: MONDAY

THE LAST SUPPER

Anyone who has visited Niagara Falls on the border of Canada and the United States will know the hypnotic effect generated by this vast cataract of water. The river flows very slowly, only gathering momentum as it reaches the lip of the falls. Then, suddenly, it surges forward and plunges hundreds of feet, down onto the rocks below.

As the disciples prepared for what was to be their last meal with Jesus, events are moving with a similar deceptive calm. Only a few details trouble us as we read the familiar accounts in the gospels, moving slowly towards the edge.

In three of the gospels, Matthew, Mark and John, the narrative of the Last Supper is preceded by a disturbing incident when Jesus is the guest at a meal. As we saw two days ago, a woman appears carrying a small bottle of very expensive perfume. There, in front of all the guests, she anoints Jesus with it. 'The whole house was filled with the fragrance,' says St John. It is a loving act, but in all three accounts there is anger at what she has done. And in all three accounts Jesus is described as confronting her attackers and praising her insight and generosity.

As he is gradually drawn towards his death, she has anointed his body for burial. As the Spirit of God anointed and empowered him for his work in the world, so the nameless woman anoints him for the finishing of that work. As he feels the touch of her hand and the moisture of the oil, he knows he is being anointed and empowered to face his coming death.

The other incident is hardly worth mentioning – except that Mark and Luke pay particular attention to it. When Jesus sends the disciples to find the place where they will hold their last meal together, he directs them to look for a man who will be carrying a water jar. What is so strange about that? Only that this was traditionally a woman's task, not a man's. Was this another hint of boundaries being crossed – of people not conforming to traditional patterns? But why mention it here? Why mention it in the gospels? Why indeed, except that it is another piece of the jigsaw – and we do well not to throw those pieces away. Instead perhaps we need to keep our eyes open for matching pieces.

Meanwhile, there are more serious developments to consider. We are so accustomed to reading the accounts of the Last Supper in the Communion service in church, or seeing the meal portrayed by the great Renaissance painters, that the event has a familiarity which blunts our perceptions.

We know Jesus and the disciples met for this meal and, while it was in progress, Jesus took bread, broke it, and gave it to them. The accounts are clear that he said words to the effect that the bread was in some way his body – not literally, but in the sense that his breaking and giving it to them to eat represented the giving of himself – both in life and in death.

Similarly, towards the end of the meal, he took a cup of wine and gave it to them with the words, 'This is my blood.' Blood, as everyone present was aware, was the symbol of life. Jesus was making it clear that, in sharing the wine with them, he was sharing his life with them. It was as though he was saying: 'Everything I am, and the life that is in me, I share with you.'

We might like to think all this was received with reverence and understanding by the 12 disciples. However, the gospels make clear this was not so. Luke says an argument arose among them at the meal as to which of them was the greatest, and all four gospel writers relate how Jesus tells the disciples that one of them will betray him. In St John's version, Jesus gives the bread to Judas and then tells him to go and do what he has to do. Judas makes the choice and it is a free choice but, having made his choice, it is as though Jesus is giving him permission to go. As though he helps him to do what he has decided to do.

But why did it happen at all? How could a person who had been so close to Jesus for so long betray him – and so unnecessarily. After all, he did not need to do it. The trap had been set by the religious authorities, and Jesus had deliberately walked into it. The authorities did not need, and did not receive, any crucial evidence from Judas on which to convict Jesus of the capital crime of blasphemy. All they needed was to find him when they decided to spring the trap. All Judas was promising to do was to lead them to him. So why did he betray his closest friend?

Reading the gospel accounts, we are struck by the fact that the betrayal is bracketed by two events. One, which we have already encountered, is the appearance of the woman with the bottle of perfume and the anger of the disciples, and Judas in particular, at the waste this involved. In the accounts of the event in both Matthew's and Mark's gospels, the incident precipitates Judas' departure to betray Jesus. But why should that make him so angry?

In St John's Gospel, we may find a clue to what was going on. In John, the act of betrayal comes at the Last Supper. His account introduces a wholly different dynamic. One of the disciples is described as being 'the one whom Jesus loved'. There is a possibility this person was John himself. We do not know what the expression 'Jesus loved' means, but it must indicate a particularly close or warm bond of friendship. This disciple is reclining next to Jesus at the supper in the favoured place – at Jesus' right side.

When Jesus tells the disciples that one of them is a traitor, about to betray him, Peter immediately wants to know who it is. He speaks quietly to the 'beloved disciple' and says: 'Ask who it is that he means.' The disciple leans back against Jesus and asks him. It is a fleeting image of close, familiar contact. An easy intimacy. Moments later Judas is gone on his murderous mission.

What is happening here? Why does someone suddenly turn against a person they respect and love? What suddenly turns love into hatred, and loyalty into betrayal – a betrayal that will destroy the other person?

One possibility is that Judas was becoming increasingly unable to cope with the generous nature of Jesus himself. Confronted by what appeared to be the reckless waste of money in the incident with the perfumed oil and being, as it is thought, the disciple responsible for the common purse, he may simply have become enraged at the disregard for common sense and prudence. Going out from that confrontation, he set in train the events which would lead to the betrayal – he negotiated the deal.

But, later, something further seems to have happened when, instead of cooling off and reflecting in the cold light of day about what he had done, he is pushed over the edge. Suddenly, at the Last Supper, it is as though he becomes consumed with a bitter anger.

There are not many things which have the power to create this bitterness towards those we have loved, but jealousy is one of them. In a sense it hardly matters, but it may have been that Judas was deeply jealous of Jesus' friendships and overt familiarity with other people. Reading through the gospel accounts, it is interesting to see how often Jesus is seen in physical contact with others.

He embraces the leper; he is touched by the woman with the haemorrhage; he makes a paste with mud and touches the eyes of the blind man in healing; he allows a prostitute to wet his feet with her tears and dry them with her hair; he touches the coffin of the dead boy outside the town of Nain; he lets a woman pour costly perfume over his head; he sits next to the disciple he loves and allows him to lean back against him; he breaks bread and says, 'This is my body'; he kneels to wash their feet.

This is a person aware of his own body and willing to be open in his physical contact with other people. Reading the account of the disciple Jesus loved, I cannot but sense an echo of my friend Aidan. Without any suggestion of a sexual relationship, it seems inconceivable that the Christ person would have been any less reserved with my gay friend than he was with these people we encounter in the gospel narratives.

Jesus would not have needed to be gay to have been able to care for and embrace someone who was; and it may well have been the disciple he loved was gay. If this was the case, then this would say something important, not about the sexuality of Jesus himself, but about an openness and acceptance of other people.

Perhaps, as with many people, Judas might have found such a situation extremely hard to accept. He may have been jealous of the special friendship he perceived between Jesus and others, both men and women. It would help us to understand a person who has been hated for 2,000 years for being human, as we are.

As we have seen, Judas did not need to betray Jesus. Ironically, he was the first to repent when he and all the other disciples, in their different ways, had failed him. He was the first person to recognize the enormity of what was happening. Matthew says he repented and went back to the authorities to try and undo what he had done. 'I have sinned and betrayed an innocent man,' he said.

What does the word of forgiveness mean here? Forgive us our sins. Or is Judas just too evil to be forgiven? Forgive us our sins, we pray and in doing so, we count Judas as one of us. Who knows, perhaps the person most reviled by the world was one of the first to be forgiven. It could go badly with us if he were not.

Day 42   Week 7
HOLY WEEK: TUESDAY
THE SERVANT KING

Mystery is an essential ingredient of a good detective story. We are given some of the clues, but not all of them. The fascination is in trying to fit the facts together to explain the mystery.

In the unfolding events of Holy Week, we are presented with a real-life mystery by St John. In his gospel he includes events which no one else seems aware of; and leaves out important facts which everyone else seems to think are essential. All three of the other gospel writers include an account of the Last Supper, in which Jesus breaks the bread and shares the wine – and commands his disciples to do this same act in remembrance of him. There are few events in the life of the Church more significant than the inauguration of the Holy Communion, which this act represents.

But, in St John's Gospel, this is not even mentioned. True, there is an account of a meal which may have been the Last Supper, but there is no reference to the bread and the wine being shared as the body and blood of Christ. This is quite amazing, since John must have been aware of the other gospel accounts, and was a person who reflected deeply on the meaning of events.

Instead of the words of the Holy Communion, however, John presents us with an event at this same meal which is hugely important – but which none of the other gospel writers seem to be aware of. Either that, or they did not think it was important enough to record. The event is the washing of the disciples' feet.

◄●►

Living in cold, damp Britain we are not very keen on feet. They are kept covered up in our shoes and socks, and are usually not in very good shape. Even on holiday on the Continent at the height of summer, we are still capable of wearing shorts, socks and trainers. We envy the Continentals with their bare, tanned feet but we would never admit it.

In the privacy of our own homes, however, we occasionally allow ourselves to walk about barefoot. We may even allow ourselves the pleasure of having our feet gently massaged by someone we love. Were we ever to go to a chiropodist, we would know the joy of having our feet cared for – the hard skin gently removed and the nails carefully pared. But we are British; and we do not like to speak of such things.

Which is a pity. Because, as people involved in reflexology and other branches of alternative medicine have discovered, the foot is very important. In some ways, it is a metaphor for the whole body. To have our feet massaged does not simply create a sense of localized well-being, it relaxes the whole body. And perhaps Jesus knew that.

In John's gospel we see Jesus sharing a meal with his disciples. It is either the Last Supper or another meal. In either case, his arrest and probable death are imminent. It is a moment of enormous significance – and tension. During the meal, says St John, Jesus gets up from the table and takes a bowl of water and a towel. He removes his outer garments and wraps the towel round him, in the manner of a Roman slave. Then he kneels and begins to wash the feet of the disciples.

It is a situation of acute confusion and embarrassment. Why is he doing this? He is performing the task of a slave; yet he is their Lord. As he moves slowly from one to the other, they are looking down on the person they have always looked up to. It is they who should be washing his feet, and Peter says so. Those waiting to have their feet washed feel an increasing unease – while those he has already washed feel that blissful pleasure of having had their feet bathed and massaged by loving hands.

The tension is broken by Peter's outburst that Jesus must not wash his feet. Jesus replies that, unless he does, then Peter is not in fellowship with him. 'Then wash my hands and my head as well,' says Peter, blundering on.

But Jesus does not need to do that. The foot is the metaphor for the whole body and the whole person has been washed, bathed, touched and blessed. We know how Peter felt about that, but what about the others? How did Judas feel as Jesus gradually worked his way round the group towards him. How did he feel as Jesus knelt before him and took those feet, which would so soon carry Judas to the authorities to betray him, and gently washed them? How did 'the beloved disciple' feel as his dear Lord washed his feet – feet which would in a few hours be standing beside a bloody cross?

Why did Jesus do it? And why did John record the event? Because Jesus was telling them something essential about God. It is not enough to tell people that God is love – we need to be shown what that means. Jesus showed them in a simple and memorable way. In an act of humility, he showed them the nature of love – that it serves. It is to the eternal credit of John that he could describe the Christ person in the most majestic language in the opening words of his gospel as nothing less than the second person of the Trinity; and, at the same time, picture this person kneeling in a hired room washing the feet of the people who were about to betray and desert him.

And John spells this out. When he has finished washing their feet, Jesus puts on his outer clothes. Then, robed and with author-ity, he gives them a commandment: 'If I, your Lord and master, have washed your feet, so you must wash each other's feet. This is my command to you: That you love one another.'

John chooses for the final act of Jesus before his arrest some-thing equally simple and important as the breaking of bread. And this act fulfils the same function – it encapsulates the meaning of God's love and enables that love to be shared. Whatever else the disciples remembered of those terrible hours before their friend's arrest, they would not forget the experience of having their feet washed. Just as they would remember the texture and taste of the bread and the wine, so too they would remember his hands bathing their feet and the solid muscle as, kneeling, he rested each foot on his leg to dry it in the towel. It was the action of a slave; but he was not their slave and his hands were loving hands.

—◆—

Looking back, centuries later, it seems so strange and yet so predictable, that the Church should have chosen the eucharistic words of the Last Supper as the central act of its worship. Day by day the priest stands, robed and with authority, at the altar and repeats the words of Christ at that meal: 'This is my body which is

given for you. This is my blood which is shed for you.' Is it a coincidence that, for almost all of those centuries, those words have
been spoken by men standing in a place of power while others
knelt? Men who have handed out not only the wafer and the wine
to the masses, but from their privileged place, have also handed
out doctrine and exercised control.

How different things might have been if, instead of placing the
eucharistic sharing of the bread and the wine at the centre of its
life, the Church had placed the washing of the disciples' feet at the
centre. If the love which is expressed through servanthood had
been the defining characteristic of the Church, and the highest
office that of the one who kneels, robed in a towel?

Perhaps, in this new millennium, the Church needs to revisit
John's powerful image of the kneeling Christ and re-examine the
meaning of its own discipleship.

Day 43   Week 7
HOLY WEEK: WEDNESDAY
GETHSEMANE

Two days ago I left home. Not permanently, you understand. Just
for a few days to think and to pray – and to concentrate on writing
the most important section of this book. To get away from the
phone and the doorbell and all the other distractions. So, for the
last 48 hours, I have been staying with my friends the nuns at their
convent at Wantage, near Oxford.

Yesterday was fine, but then I woke up in the middle of the
night. For a moment I did not know where I was. In the darkness I
felt disoriented in the unfamiliar surroundings. Feeling suddenly
unsure what I am doing here. Believing passionately in what the
book is about, but uncertain as to whether I can finish it. On the
outside, appearing confident and at ease; but, inside, quietly wishing
I was back home, safe and warm and doing ordinary tasks.

They went to a place which was called Gethsemane. And he said to them, 'Sit here while I pray.' And they sat while he went and prayed. For a long time they sat. In the dark in a place they had never been before. Feeling uncertain and disoriented. Trying to stay awake after the wine they had drunk at supper. Did they, too, say to themselves, 'Why am I here?' Did they, too, passionately believe in the Christ person? But were they also silently wishing they were safe – wanting to go home and sleep the fear away?

How long did they sit there before someone finally said, 'How much longer is he going to be? What's he doing over there?'

Did one of them steal closer to the kneeling figure and hear him praying out his pain? Sense the turmoil? See for a moment in the moonlight blood on his face; then realize it must only be sweat. When did we last sweat when we prayed?

And, slipping back to the others, did the embarrassed and confused intruder recount the dreadful sight, the words of anguish overheard? And, in their own hearts, a growing dread. A terrible weariness.

Fear, confusion, anxiety, uncertainty. These things cause fatigue. People who are homeless or living in poverty in our cities face uncertainty and anxiety. Often their lives are filled with fear. Living on the streets or in damp bed-sits, they also ask, 'Why am I here?' They, too, feel pain and are weary. They, too, want to go home and sleep the fear away. They drink to kill the pain, but there is no place called home to go.

Jesus, friend of those poor and outcast, has no place to call home either. And he, too, is feeling a great weariness. For a moment, perhaps, wanting to sleep. Wanting to be at peace. 'Father, all things are possible for thee. Remove this cup from me.' Take away this pain. Take away this ordeal.

Is he alone in the darkness, or is someone else there, too? A voice that whispers: Jesus my friend. You are tired. Sleep. All this is unnecessary. You have done enough. No need to go on. It will be so unsightly. So misunderstood.

And then, it is as though Jesus snaps back into wakefulness: 'Father, your will be done, not mine.'

Suddenly there are noises. Soldiers are approaching, led by a man whose feet Jesus has washed only hours before. The other disciples are scattering – even Peter, the one who said he would die for him. Even the one for whom he has a special caring. He is alone.

Lord, forgive us our cowardice and our falling asleep. For turning away when we are confronted by danger and injustice. For taking our rest when our sisters and brothers are abused and in pain, isolated and alone; when they are confused and wearied by the poverty we impose upon them. For not remembering that we meet you in our neighbour and, as we love them, so we love you. And as we betray them, so you are betrayed once more.

We, too, leave you alone in the darkness of Gethsemane.

Father, forgive.

◄●►

Day 44   Week 7

HOLY WEEK: MAUNDY THURSDAY
THE TRIAL

We have gone over the edge. We are in free fall. Plunging downwards, into the abyss. A few days ago things seemed so calm. The preparations for the supper. The sharing of the bread and the wine. The strange incident of the washing of the feet. There was even a tense stillness in the garden where Jesus had prayed alone.

But suddenly there were soldiers and the arrest. The disciples scattering in the darkness, each trying to save his own skin. Jesus seized and bound and taken into custody to be questioned. To help the police with their inquiries.

Years later another young man, full of life and truth, was arrested and taken into custody. To help the police with their inquiries. His name was Steve Biko. He was the leader of a non-violent student organization in South Africa called the Black Consciousness Movement. He had committed no crime, except that of teaching that black people had a value and a dignity of their own. That they must become conscious of, and affirm, who they were. That they must not allow the white system to drain them of their dignity and self-respect.

He taught that black people did not depend on white people in positions of economic and political power to give them integrity and meaning. The black person was whole and complete, independent of anything the whites were or did. They must not depend on charity handouts, whether financial, psychological or spiritual, in order to live.

In a word, he opposed the idea that all good things must trickle down the white drainpipe. Steve Biko, like Jesus before him, challenged the need for the drainpipe. And that was a dangerous thing to do. So, in early September 1977, Biko was arrested and questioned. As a result of this questioning, he suffered severe head injuries. Like Jesus, he died three days later. Like Jesus, he was 30 years old.

—•—

In the Gospel accounts of the interrogation of Jesus, there is a seemingly innocent phrase which haunts us. St Mark says they began to spit on him, and to cover his face and to strike him. Luke and Matthew describe a similar process. But why would those who were questioning Jesus cover his face? Where else have we heard that?

In accounts of the present-day torture of prisoners. The victim is blindfolded. Unable to see, she or he is unable to anticipate the next blow, which may be to the head, the face, the genitals or any other part of the body. There is a terror in violence, but an even greater terror in the violence that strikes without warning. A violence that strikes by night, in the darkness of a suffocating hood placed over the head.

But a hood is useful. The person inflicting the blow cannot see the eyes of the prisoner. The victim ceases to be a fellow human being, becoming a faceless figure – a dummy. Beating a defenceless woman or man becomes less like murder; more like beating a carpet.

And were the blows light and gentle? No, they were vicious. 'They struck his head with a reed,' says St Mark a little later. A reed? A length of cane or bamboo? A rigid piece of wood, or one which flexes as the blow is delivered to produce extra velocity and cause greater pain and damage on impact? Steve Biko suffered severe head injuries. Perhaps Jesus, his face covered, also suffered head injuries.

But there was more. St Mark says, 'plaiting a crown of thorns, they put it on him.'

Stay, for a moment, with that small word 'put' and think what it might mean. Pruning roses is a hazardous business. The thorns are sharp, even though they are quite small. A thorn, even in the coarse flesh of the hand, is painful. Thorns in the Middle East are not like those on our rose bushes – they are bigger.

The soldiers plaited a crown of these thorns and put it on his head. Did they put it on his head gently? Did they trim the sharp thorns from the inside of the crown carefully with their knives? Or did they take the crown of thorns and ram it down on his head, ripping open the soft skin of the scalp and forehead? The crown of thorns, locked on to his head, was an act of physical violence and psychological degradation.

So is that it? Has Mark finished with us; and have we finished with the bloodied Christ, at least for the time being? We have not. Mark makes two more statements. One is of overt violence and the other a half-spoken suggestion which we will find even harder to confront. First, Mark says the Roman governor had Jesus flogged. Then the soldiers took him inside the courtyard and called together the whole company.

Once more, we need to stop and reflect on what we are being told. Flogging was carried out, not with a single-strand whip, but with a multiple-strand instrument of torture. Sharp pieces of metal and bone were attached to each of the long, leather thongs. Each fragment was designed to tear open the flesh. Thirty-nine lashes were traditionally given – one less than the number commonly thought to be enough to kill a man. Jesus, his back ripped open, was being systematically beaten almost to the point of death.

But perhaps something even worse may also have happened

behind those closed doors. They called together the whole company, says Mark. They then dressed him in the royal purple – the symbolic robes of the emperor himself. What happened next?

We perhaps imagine Jesus being gently mocked by a small group of good-natured soldiers intent on nothing more than some boisterous horse-play. But a company of soldiers is not a small group. The word means battalion. They gathered together a crowd of between 200 and 600 men. Then they dressed their victim in the robes of their emperor. Did they like this emperor who ordered them to march to the ends of the earth, to endure hardship and often to die a brutal death? Perhaps some did. Others may not. And some may have vented that anger in extreme ways.

The physical abuse of prisoners is common in Britain's jails. And, although it is seldom spoken of, there is also frequent sexual abuse. It is a form of power and control in those overcrowded prisons. No matter how offensive it may seem, we cannot rule out the possibility that Jesus could have been sexually, as well as physically, abused that night.

Whatever happened, we will never know the full facts. Eventually, says Mark, they dressed him in his own clothes. Then they took him out to crucify him.

We read the gospel story every Easter. Sometimes we also read in our newspapers reports of imprisonment and torture. We read the words, but we do not hear the sounds. We do not smell the sweat or the fear. We do not see the blood and the urine. We turn away. From Steve Biko, dying from head injuries; from the men and women, tortured and abused in prison cells across the world today; and from the bloody figure of the Christ.

Father, in our shame, forgive us.

HOLY WEEK: GOOD FRIDAY
CRUCIFIXION NOW

It was a warm spring morning. The traffic flowed freely. The inter-city trains came and went on time. In their expensive offices, lawyers and accountants, chief executives and marketing managers went about their important business. Shoppers began to arrive and soon the streets were busy. In the city which prides itself on being the second most important commercial centre in Britain, life went on as usual.

Meanwhile, outside the local authority children's home the car slowed and halted. The driver wound down the window and looked across at the young girl who had just come out of the gates. He had seen her before. He was often in the area. Driving slowly; always watching.

This morning he beckoned her over to the car and spoke. After a moment's hesitation, she got in and the car drove away. No one had noticed.

Marie had been living in the children's home for almost a year. Her parents had rowed often and the social services department had finally decided she was at increasing risk. She was placed in care in the children's home. She had never known the love and security of a stable family life, and local authority care was not the place to find it.

But the man in the car spoke quietly to her. He offered to take her for a drive and to buy her nice clothes; to take her to nightclubs and to give her a good time. He offered to look after her and find her a nice place to stay. He offered her affection and friendship. But he was not a friend; he was a pimp. And he offered her drugs.

Within weeks, Marie was on heroin and increasingly dependent on him for her drugs. In a few months, she was being prostituted on the streets of the city. A year later, she tried to run away, but the man followed her and caught her. Bringing her back to the city, he beat her savagely – with a bicycle chain. She did not run away again. She was 12 years old.

Few people walking the streets of the busy city centre would dream that within a mile of the expensive offices and shops, children are abused and prostituted. Often they are imprisoned in this living hell by coercion – drugs, threats, assault, rape and, in extreme situations, torture. Only recently has child prostitution been reclassified as child abuse, thanks to the work of charities like The Children's Society.

—•—

In another city, life was going on much as normal. Not many people had heard about the arrest. Even so, a small crowd had gathered to watch. Someone said he looked pretty knocked about as he walked, carrying a section of the cross on which he would be hung. At one point he stumbled, and they got someone else to carry the heavy cross-timber. When it came to it, they tied the others onto their cross, but this one they nailed. Someone in the crowd vomited as the first nail went in. Big nails, and not very clean.

Crucifixion is a Roman method of execution. The body is stripped, then fastened to the cross-member of the scaffold and left to hang. After a time, exhausted, the victim is no longer able to support his body with his legs. The full weight is then taken on the arms. Gradually, the weight of the body constricts the lungs which are crushed inwards and the person begins to suffocate. It takes a long time, but death finally comes. As it does, the victim loses control of his bodily functions – bowels and bladder. This form of death is profoundly degrading.

But, on this occasion, there was no time to allow events to take their natural course. The following day was the Sabbath, and the Passover festival. The Jewish day begins, not at dawn, but at sunset the previous day. The authorities had hoped it would all be over by then. A soldier was dispatched to hurry things along. He broke the legs of the other two, to make sure the suffocation process did not drag on. The third one seemed already dead. To make certain, the soldier plunged a spear into the man's side, tearing deep into the internal organs. Blood came out. The man did not move.

There were some women near the cross. Someone said there was a man with them. They, too, were still.

—◦—

Centuries have washed away at Christianity until, for many people, it has changed from a rough faith to a smooth religion. Whether it is religious art and church architecture, theology or church music, the tendency has been to beautify and to harmonize. The same has been true of our traditional pictures of the cross. We see images of a man, his body clean and carefully draped, hanging on a cross. But we do not see the blood or the soiled wood. We do not hear the breathing and the pain.

We assume it was all a very long time ago, but it was not. Christ was crucified quite recently in my own city. Not with three nails and a wooden cross, but with a bicycle chain.

How easy it is to picture the Christ person as a man – calm and dignified in his encounter with death, according to the makers of stained glass windows. How hard it is to see Christ crucified in our own cities and towns by pimps and respectable men who work in offices and live in good neighbourhoods – and have a liking for little girls. We have no trouble with the image of Christ the man, but can we see the Christ as a raped and abused child, beaten with a bicycle chain?

We sing the hymn There is a Green Hill Far Away. But for many children the cross is not far away. It is upstairs in their father's bedroom. It is outside the school and the children's home where men wait in cars. For most of us, Good Friday comes once a year. For them it comes more often. And we are in the crowd.

—◦—

Meanwhile, on the hillside, all is not what it seems. In the stillness of the dying, the most profound action is taking place. 'Father, forgive them.' They were his words – his prayer. But his spoken prayer is only an articulation of what is happening. We often think of prayer and action as being separate, different. Often the religious 'life of prayer' has diverted attention away from action, encouraging a lack of action. But that is not prayer. Prayer is the articulation of love – and love is a social activity, sometimes expressing itself in stillness, but always expressing itself in action.

In the absolute stillness of a man nailed to a cross, a powerful action is in progress. The life seemingly being taken is, in fact, life being given. An extravagant gift of life poured out. 'I am laying my life down of my own free will,' says Jesus in John's gospel. 'No one has robbed me of it.'

If a man asks for your shirt, give him your coat also. But what is that about? Simply the living out of love. To find freedom for the one who gives and the one who receives. To refuse to allow yourself to engage in retribution and become an aggressor in the face of aggression, and so fuel the cycle of violence and evil. Forgiveness is about the restoration of a bond of love and goodwill; seeking the well-being, even of the person who causes you injury.

If sin means the breaking of relationship, as it does, then here Christ is, indeed, dying for the sin of the world. The separatedness and brokenness of our relationship with God. One word says it all – and it is an Abba word. The love of God the Creator is a love which cannot be negated by suffering or injustice or death. The word 'forgive' is not a request but an affirmation, just as the Crucifixion is an act of affirmation of God's love.

Meanwhile, a group of women stand nearby, watching. Were women so insignificant in that society they were not in danger of being arrested? Or were they the only ones with courage? St Luke says there were others there, but does not name any of them. Where was Peter? Where were the other men who had been so loyal to him, arguing about which of them was the most important? Where were they now?

The women, however, are there and they are named. Among them is Mary Magdalene. But, in St John's gospel, another figure appears. The disciple whom Jesus loved. He stands with Mary, the mother of Christ, near the cross. 'Mother, there is your son,' Jesus says to her. And to the disciple, 'There is your mother.' Did he really say those words, or were they a later addition by St John? We do not know – perhaps it does not matter.

Less than a mile away, in the city, everything seems normal as people prepare for the Passover festival. But, somewhere, a man is dying of remorse. He is tying a rope to a tree branch. Others are in hiding. It is not much past mid-afternoon, but a shadow has been moving swiftly towards us and suddenly the sky has turned dark.

Father, breathe forgiveness over us.

———◦➤———

Day 46 Week 7
HOLY WEEK: EASTER EVE
A DAY OF DARKNESS

Today is a day of darkness. They have gone to ground like hunted animals; hiding away for fear of the authorities. Still and silent in case someone else says, 'You were with him. You too are a Galilean.'

Half the time, while he was alive, they did not understand what he was saying. Now he is dead, they do not know what it all meant. The trial and execution happened too quickly. A few short hours ago, he was breaking bread with them and kneeling to wash their feet. Now he is cold in the grave. The hands which clenched in anger at the suffering of the poor were opened wide to receive the nails. Now they will never break bread again. The floor boards in the upper room are still dark from where the water spilled, but he will never wash their feet again. The realization has hardly begun to sink in. For weeks there will be only a sickening numbness, and a growing fear that they too will be caught and punished.

Somewhere is his mother, distraught with grief at the death of her first-born. Remembering the day of his birth and, weeks later, the day they took him to the Temple in thanksgiving. How an old man had dreamed he would not die until he had seen the Lord, the promised one. When he saw the child, he took it in his arms and wept for joy. But his tears were also for sorrow. He had told her the child was destined to be a sign that men reject. Many in Israel would stand or fall because of him. And a sword would pierce her heart also. She had not known whether to believe him; whether he was a wise man or a mad man. Today she knew. He was not mad.

---◦►---

Somewhere in the township of Guguletu, outside the beautiful city of Cape Town, overlooked by the majestic presence of Table Mountain, live six mothers. They too are distraught with grief. Their children have been caught in a police raid. All six teenage boys lie dead. A police officer is photographed standing triumphant, his rifle raised in salute. Like a big-game hunter who has shot his first lion, he stands over them, one foot placed on the bodies.

---◦►---

Somewhere in another city, the 11 remaining disciples are hiding, distraught with grief. Their lives have begun to collapse like a block of flats that is being demolished. For a few seconds after the explosion, the building seems to hang there. Then, gradually, in slow motion, it begins to collapse in on itself.

The women who stood near the place of execution are preparing to go to the tomb at first light, once the Sabbath is over. It is a foolhardy plan. They say they want to wash his body and prepare it properly for burial. They may well be arrested. The men will not go with them to open up the tomb. They say it is foolishness, but their words fall on deaf ears. They are all deaf. Deafened by the sound of a hammer on nails. Deafened by his last cry of despair, 'Father, why have you forsaken me?'

They were deaf, too, to another voice. It was there in the pain and horror of the dying. Strangely, it may have been at the point of death that we heard the first whisper of life.

One of the thieves who was being crucified with him hurled abuse at him, as though trying to create a protective shield of anger. But the other thief spoke words which were different. Turning to the Christ person hanging beside him, he said, 'Jesus, remember me when you come into your Kingdom.' If Luke has it right, he did not say, If you are the Messiah and if you come into your Kingdom. His words are words of faith and affirmation. When this happens, he says, let me be with you.

And then, from the place of death, Jesus speaks his own words of life and hope: 'You will be with me.' Even in the face of this terrible suffering, the gift of hope is offered and received. Just as the words of Psalm 22, which begin in the depths of despair, end in a cry of hope. But the disciples do not know that. The words from the cross are carried away by the wind and they are left in their cold despair.

And will we watch with them? Will we stay awake for just one day? As their sweat falls like drops of blood and perhaps they pray this cup might pass from them? Will we keep a vigil with these people in their grief? No, we will not.

For today is a day of darkness – and flower arranging.

Across the nation, we are busy preparing: 'The flowers had to be ordered, you see. Last week. Then they had to be delivered and we kept them in buckets of water in the vestry where it was cold. But we are using new oasis. No, I am afraid you cannot sit quietly in the church. We have to do the flowers. We want the church to look nice for tomorrow.'

Father, forgive.

———◄●►———

EASTER WEEK: EASTER DAY
THE LAST WORD

The trouble with Easter is it comes too soon. There is simply not enough time between the terrible events of Good Friday and the discovery of resurrection to make the necessary adjustment. It is not the fault of the Church, but Easter Sunday is in the wrong place. Like an aircraft in a steep dive, we cannot pull out in time. Plummeting down through Holy Week, we are still going down. And so are the disciples.

Men often seem to be much more limited than women when it comes to complex situations. They can be very effective at single-focus tasks – climbing a mountain or kicking a ball. But when it comes to two or more simultaneous tasks, they get confused. Women, on the other hand, seem to thrive on complexity. At any rate, the women who had been at the crucifixion and who were just as grief-stricken by the death of the Christ person, were able to carry on operating in a constructive way. In all four gospel accounts, it was the women who first went to the tomb, apparently to perform the urgent task of cleaning and embalming the body before it began to decompose.

The accounts vary about what happened next. The underlying theme is that the tomb was found to be empty; that the women went and told the disciples; that there was great confusion. Mark's gospel ends abruptly with the statement: 'They ran away from the tomb beside themselves with terror. They said nothing to anyone for they were afraid.'

Two things need to be said at this point. First, there was no expectation that the tomb would be empty or that the Christ person would in any way have been 'raised' to life. If the disciples had been expecting the Resurrection, they would not have been so dismissive of the women's story. And they might well have gone to the tomb to witness this great miracle.

Second, there seems no doubt that, whatever the Resurrection involved, it produced a massive input of energy and motivation for the disciples. From being a frightened group of grieving followers, they were in some way transformed into a joyful and confident community of faith, willing to go out and risk certain death in order to tell people about this 'resurrection' event.

People may sometimes be willing to die for an ideal, but not many are willing to die for a lie of their own making. At first the disciples were slow to grasp what appeared to be happening – further encounters with the Christ person progressively changed that.

What is remarkable is that, while it is the men who figure prominently in the gospel narratives until the crucifixion, and it is men who emerge as the leaders in the community of faith as it gradually forms itself into the primitive Church, it is the women who play the crucial role in the resurrection sequences. It is to women that the Resurrection is revealed and it is to women, and to Mary Magdalene in particular, to whom the first resurrection appearances are granted. Only in John's gospel do the men even go to the tomb.

This incident is particularly interesting because of the way in which the drama is played out. And because of the disciples who are involved. St John says Mary Magdalene goes alone to the tomb. She finds that the stone sealing the burial chamber has been moved. She runs to tell Peter and the disciple whom Jesus loved. Together, side by side, they run to the tomb. But John, the beloved disciple, runs faster than Peter and arrives first. However, instead of going into the tomb, he waits at the threshold. Peter catches up and immediately goes inside. The other disciple then follows. St John says the beloved disciple saw the body wrappings – and he believed.

Peter's relationship with the beloved disciple must, in that preceding 24 hours, have been quite strained. Peter was the leader; yet it was he who had denied and deserted Jesus in his hour of need. According to the gospel writer, however, the beloved disciple had been at the execution, standing with Mary, the mother of Jesus, near the cross.

As they ran to the tomb, it was he who got there first. What was he thinking as he ran? Perhaps he was desperately hoping the man he loved was alive. And what might Peter have been thinking as he ran? Perhaps he was hoping Jesus was dead and that his guilt at having denied Jesus had died with him. Perhaps he did not want his deep sense of shame to be resurrected.

John halted at the threshold, unable to bear to look at the body of his friend. It was as though his overwhelming emotion was one of love. Maybe Peter rushed in to see whether he was in the clear. It may have been John did not want the body to be there. But maybe Peter did.

———•———

Looking back, we can also see that Jesus' relationship and attitude to women was unusual, if not unique, in the times in which he lived. Mary Magdalene was obviously a significant person in his life – and in his death and resurrection. How interesting that the first witness of the Resurrection, the first person to bring the news to the male disciples and the first person to encounter the risen Christ, should, in later years, have been relegated to the sidelines by the Church. How ironic that the Church, which exists to live out the love of Christ, ended up being led by the man who had frequently misunderstood him, three times denied him, abandoned him at the cross and who then, perhaps, had hoped he was still dead in the tomb. How different things might have been if the Church had been structured not around the male headship of Peter, but the courageous person of Mary Magdalene.

Meanwhile, the Church remains quietly discreet about the ambiguous beloved disciple; the person who was so close in love and commitment to the Christ person that the Lord's mother was committed to his care. Jesus seems to have chosen and loved some strange friends. The Church has been more conventional.

It is easy to dismiss the institutional Church as being beyond hope. As a conservative and wealthy organization from the time of Constantine it has, as often as not, been on the side of the rich and powerful and has, on many occasions, denied the one who came to proclaim freedom for the poor and the outcast. But, if the thief received the promise of resurrection in the cross, and if we sometimes wonder whether Judas himself was not beyond the unconditional love of God, is the Church not also redeemable?

Stuck on the wall in Eve's kitchen is a fading but treasured Christmas card. It is from the Archbishop of Canterbury. Nobody made him send it and, no doubt, he has many other things to remember. But perhaps that card is a sign of hope for the Church as well as for Eve. Perhaps it is a sign that the Church is gradually being transformed by the Holy Spirit and that the love of Christ is beginning to warm its old heart. One of the things Eve and I have never quite been able to agree on is our relationship with the Church. She loves the Church. Perhaps, yet again, I need to learn from her.

—◆—

Meanwhile, in our reflections on the Lord's Prayer, there is an important word we have almost forgotten. It is the word 'Amen.' In common usage it is normally taken to indicate the end of a prayer. In fact, it means something very different. It means 'Yes.'

Yes to Jesus the Christ. Yes to God. Yes to the adventure of life. Yes to resurrection. Yes to the beloved disciple, whose sexual orientation we are not sure about. Yes to the brave woman who poured costly perfume over the condemned Lord. Yes to the women who had the courage to go to the tomb. And, no doubt, Eve would be saying, yes also to the Church. The Church has certainly and courageously said yes to her.

And perhaps that is God's last word to us on our journey. A word of hope carried by the arrow of God. A word of affirmation, encouragement and laughter. Yes.

—◆—

THE ADVENT ADVENTURE
David Rhodes

An unusual series of Advent and Christmas meditations, exploring the way Christ continues to come to us through the poorest in society. Each day is like pulling a Christmas cracker as a new aspect of our faith comes alive in a series of moving, sometimes tragic, and often amusing stories.

In company with a strange assortment of fellow travellers, including three not very wise men, a small frog, homeless people from our own streets and an ugly duckling, we make a journey with a difference to discover the meaning of Christ's birth for today.

Above the sound of the ringing shop tills and the glitter of Christmas lights we catch a glimpse of angels. But some of them are wearing ragged trousers.

'The reader is taken on a journey that is full of unpredictability, challenges, blessings and encouragements. It left me wanting more and I cannot recommend it more highly than that.'
Celebrate

'The book is very well written, full of life and a joy to read.'
Life & Work

'If you buy only one book this Christmas, then this is the one to go for.'
Reform